UNLEASHING THE POWER OF EUROPEAN INNOVATION

HOW GOVERNMENT, INDUSTRY AND SCIENCE SHARE KNOWLEDGE TO OVERCOME GLOBAL CHALLENGES

Fred Bakker

Routledge
Taylor & Francis Group
LONDON AND NEW YORK

Designed cover image: Getty Images

First published 2024
by Routledge
4 Park Square, Milton Park, Abingdon, Oxon OX14 4RN

and by Routledge
605 Third Avenue, New York, NY 10158

Routledge is an imprint of the Taylor & Francis Group, an informa business
This edition brokered through Monday 9:15 Author Services, Rotterdam NL

British Library Cataloguing-in-Publication Data
A catalogue record for this book is available from the British Library

Library of Congress Cataloging-in-Publication Data
Names: Bakker, Fred (Alfred), author.
Title: Unleashing the power of European innovation: how government,
industry and science share knowledge to overcome global challenges / Fred Bakker.
Description: Abingdon, Oxon; New York, NY: Routledge, 2024. |
Includes bibliographical references and index.
Identifiers: LCCN 2023051641 (print) | LCCN 2023051642 (ebook) |
ISBN 9781032703367 (hardback) | ISBN 9781032703374 (paperback) |
ISBN 9781032703381 (ebook)
Subjects: LCSH: Technological innovations—Europe. |
Entrepreneurship—Europe. | Sustainable development—Europe.
Classification: LCC HC240.9.T4 B355 2024 (print) |
LCC HC240.9.T4 (ebook) | DDC 338.94/06—dc23/eng/20240222
LC record available at https://lccn.loc.gov/2023051641
LC ebook record available at https://lccn.loc.gov/2023051642

ISBN: 978-1-032-70336-7 (hbk)
ISBN: 978-1-032-70337-4 (pbk)
ISBN: 978-1-032-70338-1 (ebk)

DOI: 10.4324/9781032703381

Typeset in Bembo
by codeMantra

A website with cases, updates and more information is available at sharingbrainpower.eu

UNLEASHING THE POWER OF EUROPEAN INNOVATION

The world is at a critical juncture where our industrial and economic principles have to be reshaped. Three major transitions are underway: towards the use of alternative energy sources, towards carbon-neutral and sustainable production and towards digitalised manufacture and distribution. This book explores the ways in which these transitions are taking place in Europe.

No single institution can bring about the necessary changes: a productive cooperation between government, industry and (technological) knowledge centres has to be established. In this insightful book, Fred Bakker paints a vivid picture of a wide range of European businesses, industries and research institutes, joining forces to further the transitions. This process of 'Sharing Brainpower' proves to be a unique European strength that needs to be recognised and furthered.

Structured in five parts, the book provides a thumbnail sketch of Europe's goals and methods, through a bird's eye view across current initiatives towards the three transitions, to a concluding part in which the workings of Sharing Brainpower are described in terms of a set of 'lessons learned'. It shows how top-down initiatives and the bottom-up approach reinforce one another, with case stories that prove that diversity does not have to mean fragmentation; it is a source of strength.

Policymakers, industry advisers, board members, chief innovation officers and students will find much to inspire them and their work in this book.

A website with cases, updates and more information is available at sharingbrainpower.eu.

Fred Bakker spent his working life as a journalist specialising in monetary and financial affairs with *Het Financieele Dagblad* – the Dutch equivalent of *Financial Times* – serving as deputy editor, editor in chief and CEO. In addition to his writing and editing duties, he helped develop the company from a newspaper publisher to a multimedia company. Nowadays, he writes about the intersection of technology, innovation and governance strategy.

Dedicated to Frances, Jake and Duco

CONTENTS

FOREWORD

THE EUROPEAN CHALLENGE

By Antoine van Agtmael

A SECRET INGREDIENT

The basic message of Fred Bakker's new book is that there is something quite unique about Europe's innovation model that gives it a leg up in the global race for innovation. He is right and prescient to argue that collaboration – what he calls 'Sharing Brainpower' – is key to smart innovation because it requires not only brilliance, focus and persistence but also this 'secret ingredient' as a catalyst.

Europe manages to make innovation more effective by creating smart ecosystems rather than keeping knowledge to themselves, connecting like-minded partners in the corporate and research worlds and bringing start-ups inside the 'tent.' The European Commission has chosen to compete not by trying to duplicate where others are ahead, or doing everything in-house, but by betting on the green energy and digital industries of the future, by selecting 'flagship' areas. It relies on many public-private research partnerships like Germany's Fraunhofer Institute. It has also kept its eye on the need to create a modern workforce through work-study partnerships.

Building on ideas from *The Smartest Places on Earth,* which we co-authored, Fred goes one step further as he uses numerous vivid examples to illustrate how these European and national research institutes play a uniquely European role in Sharing Brainpower.

WORKING HARD AND SMART

Fred's new book starts with the recognition that there is a global race for innovation and that Europe was at risk of falling behind the United States and China with, respectively, their strong start-up culture and relentless ambition.

Fred describes how today Europe is working hard and smart to survive and prosper in the global race for innovation by focusing like a laser on the industries that make the world economy tick in the 21st century. Its data privacy legislation may annoy tech companies but is a model for the rest of the world. Europe understands that it needs to regain data sovereignty through various kinds of 'European clouds.'

It is also developing clear markers for success in achieving climate and other goals that can guide the next generation of goals. With the European Commission as conductor, a new energy chain is being created, including offshore wind parks, sun-powered electricity, hydrogen, a new generation of batteries and 'greener" nuclear by recycling the long-lasting waste. After all, global warming is starting to hit in earnest, and we have little choice but to transform life as we know it from 100+ years of addiction to fossil fuels for energy to new, sustainable sources.

THE EUROPEAN CHALLENGE

In 1968, Jean-Jacques Servan-Schreiber's book *The American Challenge* caused a sensation by focusing on the 'American challenge' in economic competition. Servan-Schreiber accurately predicted the computer revolution and (some form of) the internet. His book shocked the general public, business leaders and policymakers in Europe into refocusing policies on greater integration and more creative innovation.

Contrary to Schreiber's fears, the European economy did not bankrupt itself or become a 'museum' but proved to be resilient and successful, not least because some of his recommendations were followed. Today, the multinationals highlighted in *The American Challenge* like IBM, GM, Westinghouse or Union Carbide are no longer leading their industries nor are they at the forefront of innovation. American multinationals only produce 4% of the European Union's GDP (with European multinationals having a nearly similar share of the American economy).

But in the light of the new generation of big American companies like Alphabet, Amazon, and Tesla that came out of nowhere to dominate their markets, it is easy to overlook European successes in global markets and innovation. Europe's multinationals play leading and innovative roles in the semiconductor machinery (ASML), laser (Trumpf), wind energy (Ørsted), robotics (ABB, Stäubli, Kuka, Comau), aerospace (Airbus), pharmaceutical and biotech (Bayer, Crispr, BioNTech). Many others in the car, chemical, appliance, retail, luxury goods and agricultural industries have transformed themselves into world-class players.

A MODEL FOR THE WORLD?

Fred's book could have been called *The European Challenge*. Just like *The American Challenge*, his book is a 'call to arms' and may cause similar shockwaves, especially now that the invasion of Ukraine has brought a painful reminder that only close collaboration and a joint defence strategy can keep Europe strong. The battle for innovation is heating up at the same time as globalisation is being replaced by a world of two dominant blocs of China-Russia and the United States-European Union-Democratic Asia.

As is made clear in this book, Europe's network of public-private research institutes can be a model and catalyst for the rest of the world in its proven ability to 'Share Brainpower' and will play a crucial role in Europe's ambitious innovation agenda that is focused on 21st-century needs.

Antoine van Agtmael is senior adviser at Foreign Policy Analytics, a public policy advisory firm in Washington DC. He is also a Board member of, among others, The Brookings Institution and the NPR Foundation.

INTRODUCTION

A WORK IN PROGRESS

NEW ECONOMIC MODELS

In my previous book, *The Smartest Places on Earth*, which I wrote with Antoine van Agtmael, I coined the term 'Sharing Brainpower'. I had signalled a growing trend of companies, universities, startups and local authorities forming alliances to handle new and complex technologies. It was Gerard Kleisterlee, the former CEO of Philips who brought me to this concept. I had lunch with him sometime in the early years of this century. At the time, I was editor-in-chief of *Het Financieele Dagblad*, and he was the freshly appointed CEO of Philips. His board had shortly before made the decision to change the world-famous but private think tank NatLab into an open research campus, to which even competitors could be invited.

My question to him was why this openness was necessary. And his answer was simple: technology is advancing to become increasingly complex, and no single company can possess all knowledge required to create the next generation of products. You need other companies and knowledge institutions to share knowledge: *Sharing Brainpower.*

After that lunch, that remark kept spinning in my head. If this sharing of knowledge was indeed to become standard practice, it would have far-reaching consequences for the structure of our economy. This would improve the quality of the supply side

DOI: 10.4324/9781032703381-1

considerably; something that economists and the modellers did not yet take into account. I had noticed something similar when the Dutch government implemented austerity measures in the 1980s, causing the models to predict a severe negative effect on economic growth. But in reality, the policy resulted in a stock market boom that benefited many private individuals who converted the capital gain into the purchase of a new TV or even a new home. So I asked decision-makers at the central bank whether this dynamic was reflected in the models. A few years later, the models were indeed adjusted and the value development of investments in securities and real estate taken into account in consumer demand.

Although I had studied political science and economic theory in Amsterdam, as a journalist I was constantly wondering what was really happening in the economy and in society, and why these events were not predicted by economic models. I was constantly researching how structures and cultures change. With this new book, I used the same approach, and so I asked myself the question: How does Europe go about innovating and how does Europe organise change?

Let me give you an example of how these topics played with me early on. It must have been at the end of 1982 that I was present as a financial editor at a discussion between a member of the Executive Board of the Bundesbank and a top official of the French Ministry of Finance. A year earlier, the socialist François Mitterrand had been elected president with the promise of getting the economy back on track through additional spending. In a study centre just outside Frankfurt, the knives were sharpened because, in the eyes of the Bundesbank, an irresponsible policy was being pursued in Paris.

The emotions were palpable, the criticism was unsalted and the defence was predictable. But sitting there as an observer in the front row, I realised that something unique was happening here. Half a century before, this disagreement would have caused a diplomatic riot and deterioration of bilateral relations. Now the countries could fall back on a legal construct, the EMS, which regulated monetary relations.

A few months later, the bomb dropped. In March 1983, the French franc declined in value relative to the Deutsch-mark. There was a lot of spectacle over the weekend in which the adjustment was made, but the conversation about improving the mechanism continued – eventually leading to the establishment of the Euro currency.

NEW EUROPEAN STRUCTURES

Europe is a legal construct that brings countries together, forcing consultation and coordination that lead to a further refinement of the structure. As editor-in-chief, I came into contact with the new members from Central Europe as a board member of the European Business Press. What struck me in the conversations with them was the fear and disgust towards the former coloniser and the desire to shape their regained freedom. Only after the Russian invasion of Ukraine did I begin to understand what it must have been like to live in that fear. I believe their presence as new member states will bring Europe to greater balance and maturity.

This book is about how we continue to build Europe. How diversity can lead to more unity and dynamism. In *The Smartest Places on Earth*, we were fascinated by the resilience of old industrial regions where local government, universities and businesses could achieve new growth by sharing their knowledge. Sharing Brainpower was the cure. The European Commission makes alliance building the backbone of 21st-century industrial policy. Here, too, Sharing Brainpower is the cure. The commission sees the need to share knowledge in order to get the transitions to sustainability and energy efficiency off the ground. The same goes for the third transition, which is towards a safe and independent digitisation of European business.

The question is, how is this top-down approach taken up by member states, regions, research institutions, companies and funders? The commission does not impose its will, but leaves it to the member states to give their own interpretation to Sharing Brainpower. And that leads to roughly three types of approaches.

- The first is what I call the 'Nordic Approach', in which the government is not in the spotlights, but provides a clear vision of (in this case) sustainability. Companies and knowledge institutions can trust this long-term commitment and build ecosystems around it.
- Second, there is the 'Paris Connection', in which the government openly directs. There is close consultation on who works together with whom. State aid is widely available. Where necessary, corrective action is taken.
- And finally, there is the 'Berlin Bridge', a federative tradition of cooperation. Knowledge and consultation are central; if parties come to a head, the chancellor is the referee. The Industry 4.0 initiative is a good example of this model.

The commission does not have a preferred approach. Rather, she is a conductor who wants to let the different sections in the orchestra come into their own, focusing first on harmony. The commission is giving impetus to the emergence of new markets. It takes care of the legislation it submits to the member states and the European Parliament, and it keeps a close eye on the optimal functioning of the internal market. This is how new forms of cooperation take shape.

ABOUT THIS BOOK

This book is structured in five parts, working from a thumbnail sketch of Europe's goals and methods, through a bird's eye view across current initiatives towards the three transitions, to a concluding part in which the workings of Sharing Brainpower are described loosely in terms of a set of 'lessons learned'. This latter part can help decisionmakers, industry leaders and think tanks come to grips with the principle and make it work in their respective situations.

As you will see throughout the descriptions of current initiatives, technological challenges are very much shaping and propelling the ways; different parties are seeking out each other's expertise. This harks back to the initial comment by Philips CEO Kleisterlee. The three transitions in European industry are dependent on finding technological answers to questions on CO_2 and energy conservation/renewal, digitisation and recycling.

PART I

FORGING A FUTURE-PROOF UNION

1

EUROPE

COMING TO ITS OWN

CRISES AS ENGINES FOR CHANGE

In the last decades, European policymakers have turned into crisis managers. The heads of government in the European Council, in particular, repeatedly became entangled in complex discussions about how Europe should proceed – or how we had to say goodbye to each other. These heated discussions have often strengthened Europe, but this strength is a reactive ability, with compromise as its best outcome. Worse still, when the pressure of a crisis was removed, the political will to carry out necessary improvements often disappeared. Crises became the engine of change.

The move towards crisis management is mainly due to new accents that the European Commission has placed in its policy approach. In recent years, it has increasingly focused on identifying and exploring weaknesses and dependencies facing the European economy and society. This creates a sense of urgency, a proactive attitude – as was shown when the EC set up its own battery chain and drafted the Chips Act, which should bring the production of 'smart chips' to Europe. The commission invites politicians, entrepreneurs and scientists and asks them to form alliances that combine knowledge and industrial execution power, which can turn a trailing position into a leading one.

DOI: 10.4324/9781032703381-3

SOVEREIGNTY AS A GUIDING PRINCIPLE

In a very short time, the word sovereignty has entered the European vocabulary. The nationalistic attitude of US President Trump provoked European policymakers that we must learn to stand on our own two feet. But it was mainly Covid and the war in Ukraine, which delicately exposed the dependencies and showed our vulnerabilities.

For a long time, Western politicians have thought that international trade would lead to mutual understanding. Trade with Russia would deter the Kremlin from national extremism, and rapid economic development in China would gradually lead to a democratisation of the political system. Moscow and Beijing have made it clear that they do not want to live in such a unipolar world. They choose to determine what happens in their direct spheres of influence. But their spheres of influence are gradually being extended; both have tempted countries to invest in infrastructure works on favourable terms. Russia obviously took a more drastic approach to extension.

Europe needs to address this reality: Covid and the war in Ukraine have shaken us up, and not just in a political way. In 2020, it turned out that we had outsourced so rigorous work that masks were no longer made in Europe. China had become the Workshop of the World, we said admiringly. They did the work which had become too expensive in the West. But when China started to implement a zero-Covid policy and entire cities were closed off, there was suddenly a lack of chips and other parts and goods. Our outsourcing strategy had been too one-sidedly focused on one country. But re-installing factory work here is a complex, time-consuming and costly affair. Still, it suddenly became a serious option.

China aims to be a world leader in robotics, autonomous cars, quantum computing and AI by 2049. The realisation that these are not pipe dreams quickly dawned on European policymakers. Suddenly, Europe experienced its vulnerability if the standards were being set in Beijing. Now, legislation is being drawn up in Brussels that should protect technology and tech companies from Chinese investors.

When Russia attacked Ukraine in 2022, Europe closed ranks. Economic sanctions followed that would isolate Russia; the new pipeline that would supply Germany with even more Russian natural gas was not commissioned. The war led to unrest in the energy market, with unprecedented price increases as a result. We were made all too aware how addicted citizens and businesses had become to cheap fossil fuels. The search for alternative suppliers and the switch from fossil to renewable energy sources was no longer a goal that could be achieved in 20 years. A political emergency was needed to accelerate the energy transition.

The war in Ukraine has also highlighted that European countries are deficient in the defensive, and even more so in the offensive military sense. With its precision and sensor-controlled weapons, including drones, the USA proved once again how effectively it can operate with the latest technological applications. Europe is lacking here, and too dependent on the USA. It is up to the European Commission to decide what spending and research it wants to allocate to boost technological experience in this field.

UNITY INCREASES STRIKING POWER

Covid and the war in Ukraine have strengthened coherence in EU policy and its implementation. After some difficulties, the commission emerged as the purchaser of vaccines for all member states. In addition, at the request of the heads of government, the European Commission came up with a Covid Recovery Plan which, with a budget of 750 billion Euro, should ensure a sustainable transition.

Brussels' appeal and guideline to set up alliances, as a means to realise the above transitions, is surely an ambitious one. Will it work? Analysts and policymakers ask questions in which both enthusiasm and cynicism can be heard. Can you control this process from above? Will this create another bureaucratic maze; is it not wiser to leave the adjustments to the markets? How will corruption be fought? Do we have to put all that money into new technology that will only benefit companies? Is the new industrial policy just a drop in the ocean; have we already missed the boat and are China and the US unassailably ahead?

I am not one of those cynics who think it's too late for Europe. At a time when the geopolitical situation is constantly changing, when there is uncertainty about the nature of new technological tools and the pace at which they become available, there is a need for policies underpinned by a vision. The commission sees the sharing of knowledge and the pooling of forces as an indispensable tool for creating unity in diversity.

I obviously commend that choice, but its implementation requires more than giving people money and putting them into digital innovation hubs. Bringing people, companies and knowledge institutions together must meet a number of conditions, so that the process does not get bogged down in bureaucratic procedures. Later on, I will highlight what can we learn from the sharing of knowledge that companies and regions have already realised.

2

SHARING BRAINPOWER

A EUROPEAN APPROACH

FOCUS, INITIATIVE AND CONNECTIONS

In this book, I am building on the research that Antoine van Agtmael and I did for *The Smartest Places on Earth*. We looked for regions and cities in the US and Europe that were able to achieve new economic quality and growth with an ecosystem of Sharing Brainpower. Old industrial centres, the so-called Rustbelts, turned out to be able to grow into 'Brainbelts.'

Antoine and I learned a number of lessons from the many conversations we had with entrepreneurs, philanthropists, professors, scientists and local politicians. In the first place, there usually was a sense of despondent urgency. People were at a loss, lacked perspective and hope for improvement. The existential need to change was great. This ties in with the EC's change into crisis management policymakers.

In a situation like that, there must be people who keep a clear head. People who have a vision with which a seemingly unattainable goal can be pursued. These people also have to have a strong focus and perseverance, because in their environment there is often cynicism about plans being proposed.

You also need people who take the initiative. There is no waiting for an official sanction from the government; a region or city usually will take matters into its own hands. In Portland, Oregon,

DOI: 10.4324/9781032703381-4

for instance, philanthropist Phil Knight, founder Nike, provided the financial support that allowed the extensive cancer research by the local university hospital to be carried out in conjunction with Intel.

In Akron, Ohio, once the Rubber City of the US where Goodyear made the tyres for the Detroit auto industry, university president Luis Proenza took the lead in turning Ohio into the Polymer State. A wide range of new applications, from coatings for the steel industry to lightweight prostheses, led to new collaborations between companies and universities.

These clear-headed, driven individuals are usually very good in a third capacity: they know how to find and engage the right decision-makers, investors, technology experts and planners. These Connectors, as I call them, are crucial to the success of any brainsharing alliance. Often, the qualities are united in a single person; sometimes they are several, as in a well-balanced start-up team.

SMART ALLIANCES: SOME EXAMPLES

When I continued alone, my own research in Europe provided other examples of how cooperation between companies and universities was successfully realised. In Friedrichshafen, southern Germany, the automotive parts company ZF, in collaboration with the University of Freiburg, developed an internal data lab that has become a melting pot of ideas and technologies. The university was the engine behind this process.

In Munich, BMW founded the 'Startup Garage,' which invites start-ups to work *within the company,* together with their future internal customers. In addition, the car company has started an extensive collaboration with Intel and its subsidiary MobilEye for research on autonomous cars.

In Drachten, a small industrial town in the north of the Netherlands, some companies decided to address the consequences of new technology. The engine behind this alliance was the local branch of Philips. Kor Visscher, then a board member, invited fellow board members from a local company to a cup of coffee and shared his vision of the alliance. This personal approach proved a successful way to get everyone involved energised.

But this Connector does not open the doors to anyone. Says Visscher: 'Selection of new participants is strict. They must have a research tradition. We then talk to various company officials. People from marketing, commerce, finance, human resources and technical researchers are reviewed. The alliance should not become a CEO's plaything.' The advantage of this approach is that all people interviewed later participate in the alliance's project groups, so that consequences and possibilities are looked at from various angles. 'Only policy makers are barred from these meetings, because they should not get bogged down in administrative proceedings.'

In recent years, the group has grown to include more than 20 companies. The University of Groningen, vocational training schools and the regional government all participate in the alliance. There is still a strong focus when taking on new projects. At the same time, Visscher has made sure from the start that all participants propose projects, to avoid the alliance becoming a Philips project in all but name.

ECOSYSTEMS BUILT AROUND APPLIED RESEARCH INSTITUTES

The ground for the alliance formation called for by the commission is fertile. In the above examples, local universities played a big role. Europe has its equivalent, the applied research institutes. After the Second World War, they were founded to provide small businesses with the latest production techniques. They still are the bridge builders between universities and the business community. A tour of the institutes shows that in the last decades, they have simultaneously consolidated internally and strengthened the ties with participating companies through decentralisation.

In the 1990s, the Swedish government took the initiative to merge the 15 smaller institutes into one. This is how RISE came into being, headquartered in Gothenburg near the Chalmers University of Technology. In the meantime, the two institutes have combined research into electric transport in SEEL (the Swedish Electric Transport Laboratory) and are cooperating with SAAB, Volvo and battery producer NorthVolt.

In the industrial north-west of Spain, eight research institutes sought each other out and formed Technalia in 2011. It is working with Bilbao-based Siemens-Gamesa towards making windmills more sustainable, and research is being carried out into floating windmill parks.

Applied research institutes have understood that they must be located close to the companies involved. In Germany, Fraunhofer has 72 branches spread across the country. There are collaborations with universities, such as in Munster, where research is being done on the battery of the future.

In France, CEA, the Alternative Energies and Atomic Energy Commission with large research facilities in Paris and Grenoble, has developed the 'factory of the future.' In a Peugeot branch near Metz, the digital platform was tested together with 11 partners. In addition, CEA has developed a cooperation concept for regional technology transfer centres. Regional governments, knowledge institutes and companies can submit a proposal to CEA.

In the Netherlands, TNO, together with the industrial employers and the Ministry of Economic Affairs, launched a similar initiative, the Fieldlab. Companies, regional authorities and knowledge institutions can submit a proposal to the Ministry. After approval, the central government supplies a budget. TNO mainly plays a coordinating supporting role.

The European Commission has followed this example of Sharing Brainpower with the Digital Innovation Hubs that are being rolled out in all 27 member states. Out of more than 280 submissions, 220 proposals were approved. Regional governments, companies, start-ups and knowledge institutions are working together. The idea is to set up a network that facilitates international digital and industrial cooperation. Every country was also asked to include at least one candidate in the field of Artificial intelligence.

AN OVERVIEW OF TECHNOLOGICAL FIELDS

Batteries

Over 80% of batteries are made in Asia. The widespread introduction of electric cars prompted the EC in 2017 to invite the energy sector, researchers, entrepreneurs and knowledge institutions to set up a battery chain together.

Member states responded enthusiastically, but each in its own way. In Sweden, the government had already set up an ecosystem in Gothenburg, and Peter Carlsson, an entrepreneur who had worked at Tesla, was able to raise the necessary funds to build a factory in the north of the country. This was the start of NorthVolt.

France and Germany had openly lobbied the commission to relax state aid restrictions, allowing the French and German economic ministers to announce at a joint press conference the construction of two factories for which 500 million Euro was made available. In addition, the German federal government, together with its *Bundesländer*, promised support to researchers and companies.

Wind energy

Successful implementation of wind energy in the North Sea is the fruit of Danish company Orsted's work. The Danish government had supplied the clear political goal that fossil fuels should disappear within 30 years. Orsted's management reacted by increasing the productivity of its windmills, with experience and input from its suppliers. Sharing Brainpower proved very effective here; the company is now leading the way in generating sustainable electricity and now wants to convert excess wind energy into hydrogen.

Hydrogen

Shell and Siemens have presented ambitious plans to build their own wind farms and possibly generate hydrogen on-site. The commission picked up on this signal and, under the leadership of

Commissioner Frans Timmermans, the Hydrogen Europe initiative was launched.

New chemical industry

In the Netherlands, seven universities are working on building an E-refinery, which will allow chemistry to say goodbye to the refining and use of oil and gas as a raw material. The collaboration was set up by the Dutch research council NWO and supported by Shell, Orsted, Tata Steel and Dow Chemical.

Smart chips

Finally, the commission decided that the production of smart chips in Europe was trailing. It asked decision-makers from the sector whether Europe could acquire this knowledge alone or whether foreign companies such as Intel or TSMC, should set up factories here. A unique public discussion took place, under the guidance of ASML, the world's leading supplier of the machines with which smart chips are made. They were against developing that knowledge alone. When the Chips Act was presented by the commission and a non-European company put forward, ASML followed up with a comprehensive plan of action, showing Brussels what exactly was needed to implement this ambitious plan.

THE EC AS CONDUCTOR OF THE EUROPEAN ORCHESTRA

European industrial policy takes shape in the internal market, where strict competition rules apply and state aid is limited to prevent unfair competition. The commission shall monitor compliance with the rules and any possible relaxation, for instance, by means of the 'Important Project of Common European Interest' measure. For hydrogen, chips and batteries, the rules have been relaxed.

The exuberant subsidy policy with which Washington wants to achieve sustainability threatens to trigger a migration of European 'Green' companies to the USA. The European Commission has responded by increasing the scope for state aid until 2025. This mainly concerns state aid to battery and windmill producers. In addition, there is a unique possibility that subsidies offered by a US state may be compensated by a European country.

The commission has to negotiate between the wishes of countries that want more room for state aid and those that do not have the financial resources to provide that aid. In this, the Committee is like the conductor of an orchestra who must understand the art of having all sections play in harmony and working out the false notes.

3

KNOWLEDGE CENTRES

FROM IDEATION TO APPLICATION

A SHORT HISTORY OF EUROPEAN KNOWLEDGE CENTRES

Applied science institutes are a typical European phenomenon; they form the bridge between universities and industrial companies. Their formation history is unique in each country, but taking the CEA in France as a first case history, we can note some general trends.

In France after the Second World War, the atomic knowledge of the Curie family was built upon. The *Commissariat à l'énergie atomique* (CEA) became the founder of the later nuclear power plants, which still produce about 70% of French electricity. In the early years of its existence, the institute was more of an extension of the scientific world than a bridge builder to business.

The CEA expanded its field of activity when a branch was opened in Grenoble in 1967 where the focus of research shifted towards the then new information technology. The wish to gain knowledge about a potentially groundbreaking concept (for government and business) was paramount. Research in Grenoble soon led to a startup (as we would call it today), which grew into the Italian-French chip company STMicroelectronics. Later, the CEA entered into another international collaboration with Fraunhofer, CSEM, which emerged from the Swiss watch industry in 1984, and Finnish VTT. The alliance focused research on miniaturisation and system integration of the computer chip.

DOI: 10.4324/9781032703381-5

Only after broadening research activities and international cooperation did the CEA focus on the needs of businesses in the French region. A digital platform was built. Near Metz, Peugeot had the scoop: a test facility of the Factory of the Future was set up with more than ten suppliers.

CEA only became a real bridge builder when it responded positively to the request of regional governments to set up knowledge transfer centres. The regions had a direct interest in injecting knowledge into local businesses. The regions, together with other knowledge institutions and companies, submit a proposal, take on part of the funding and indicate the focus of the research.

The CEA continues to be reticent and service-oriented in its approach. This is characteristic of the French view on science and knowledge institutes, and for a long time, this was also the way other research centres in the rest of Europe operated. Meanwhile, some institutes have become more outward-looking and proactive.

TNO: BORN OUT OF TECHNOLOGICAL 'EMERGENCIES'

The Dutch TNO institute has its roots in the 1930s, when a group of scientists combined their expertise to come up with technology to 'hear' oncoming enemy aircraft sooner. In the decades following, TNO was often called upon by the Dutch government to spearhead or organise research into new technology; usually when some urgency was involved, such as the Second World War and the Flood of 1953. In the 70s, with various technological issues emerging from the mobility explosion and energy shortages, TNO was again the go-to research partner.

At present, TNO's fields of expertise are infrastructure and logistics, defence, circular economy and energy transition, health, and ICT and high tech. TNO, originating in Delft at the technological university, but with many locations around the Netherlands, is also heavily invested in Sharing Brainpower with the Eindhoven (Philips) region.

In 2005, for instance, TNO and its Belgian counterpart IMEC decided to form a platform for companies and universities at the High Tech Campus in Eindhoven. And so, with input from

Philips Research – for many decades one of the Netherlands' biggest and most profitable companies – the Holst Centre was born. Research work focuses on the fields of flexible electronics and wireless sensor technology. At present, 180 researchers work at the Centre, which has 56 industrial partners and 45 ongoing projects.

Another project in Eindhoven is the 'solar alliance' or Solliance. This started out as a shared research centre on thin-film solar energy with partners from the Netherlands, Belgium and Germany. But Solliance really took off once the EC changed its state-aid rules in 2014. Now, Sharing Brainpower is possible not just within the lab environment, but also in collaboration with industry partners. This seemingly minor liberalisation of aid policy by the commission opens the door to working even more intensively with and for business.

FIELDLAB: ON-THE-GROUND RESEARCH AND BUSINESS COOPERATION

In 2014, through Connector Egbert-Jan Sol, working on behalf of TNO in Eindhoven, TNO came into contact with industry leadership and officials of the Ministry of Economic Affairs. Their question was how to accelerate the digitalisation of the industry. A possible model could be found in Germany, where the digitalisation of the industrial internet had resulted in the 'Industry 4.0' project, in which companies, regional governments, knowledge institutions and applied scientific institutions such as Fraunhofer still participate.

Sol was in favour of bringing companies and local and regional governments together in projects, but he also wanted to involve knowledge institutions, be it a vocational school or a university. This new type of collaborative project was named Fieldlab (Heide, 2016).

Fieldlabs have become a way to get companies, knowledge institutions and local governments to (financially) commit to joint innovation programs, in which seasoned engineers and scientists work side-by-side with students. Participants are strongly connected to the project; Ministry officials have by now built up good experience with co-financing these projects, so they do not need justification for every individual project. This greatly enhances the flexibility of Fieldlabs.

Initiators are asked to choose a theme within the top sectors, as defined by the Dutch Ministry of Economic Affairs. Each is required to contribute financially to the project as well. The Ministry assesses the proposals. The first ten, started in 2014 and focusing on robotics, big data, composites and new cutting techniques, were awarded Fieldlab status. The partners invested a combined 3 million euros in each lab, for a maximum period of five years.

As of 2021, there are 45 Fieldlabs around the Netherlands. Around 1,000 companies are involved, sharing all their know-how as well as investing in the projects. Total investment amounts to 391 million euros, of which the private sector holds about 156 million (in 600 projects). Many Fieldlabs also have training and workshop facilities, catering to around 5,000 people each year since 2019.

WORKING WITH EVERYBODY BUT OTHER KNOWLEDGE CENTRES

With the success of the Dutch Fieldlabs in mind, the European Commission started to provide opportunities for the construction of Fieldlabs. But when, in 2019, Brussels asked European knowledge centres directly to work together, expecting a growing demand from the business community for test facilities such as cleanrooms and laboratories, it was met with resistance. Why was this? Their reluctance may partially be explained by the above description of the CEA's character, which holds true for many others.

Four institutes in Northern Europe decided to undertake a study of how cooperation could be achieved in their region. The Danes took on the role of notes keeper and their report was published in early 2020 (Danish Technological Institute, 2020). The study focused on the digital-economic and bio-economic sectors. The different forms of working together, called 'innovation ecosystems,' were put on a scale ranging from 'informal' to 'full merger.' Informal cooperation turned out to be the preferred situation, based, according to all those interviewed, on a high level of mutual professional appreciation.

The report is couched in terms that make it clear many knowledge centre leaders are walking on eggshells. World developments and the new demands they make on business, society and government alike are recognized – but each institution is afraid that committing to a particular technological solution could mean their autonomy would be lost. So each continues to build relationships within its own regional circle of companies.

BUILDING ON YOUR OWN STRENGTHS

Perhaps the wish for a truly pan-European cooperation runs counter to the way many research institutes work, and work best. Many have a regional or national reach at best. For close cooperation and alignment with smaller to medium businesses, this is probably understandable. But adding to that is the fact, alluded to in the Danish report, that many research centres historically have their roots in specific technologies.

Finland's **VTT**, for instance, focuses it research primarily on the consequences of digitalisation on society and industry. Nokia (5G), Kone (lifts) and Wärtsilä (ship engines) know how to find their way to VTT. Joint research into the effects of digitalisation has led to Kone being seen as an expert and advisor on mobility within offices and hospitals, rather than maker of lifts and escalators. Wärtsilä profiles itself as a supplier of 'sea miles,' a system which makes pay-per-mile possible.

In Norway, with its huge oil and gas reserves under the North Sea, research carried out by **Sintef** mainly focuses on nautical studies and the safe and efficient transport of oil and gas via one pipeline from various offshore fields to the mainland. Sintef has the biggest laboratories in the world in both these research areas.

Denmark is the European leader in wind energy. Together with Vestas and the University of Aarhus, **DTI** is researching sustainable materials for rotor blades. It is also focuses its research on improving the fine-tuning of robots on the work floor at Vestas. The wind turbine manufacturer thought that much of the hand work could not be taken over by robots. But eyes were opened with the introduction of the mobile robot, which takes parts from the warehouse to the factory where assembly takes place; the potential for further digitalisation of the production process is now recognised.

In Sweden, Technical University Chalmers has combined forces in the area of electric mobility. Clients Volvo, Scania and the start-up NorthVolt, which is building a gigabattery factory, are breathing life into the ecosystem. The push for this development was given at the end of the last century by the Swedish government. A wide selection of more than 15 research institutions were merged under the name **RISE.** Its head office was located in Gothenburg and in the subsequent restructuring, the focus turned on five themes including bio-economy/health and security/transport. When the Swedish parliament passes a law aimed at reducing the number of road accident deaths to zero, this became an extra impulse for RISE and Volvo to encourage research into self-driving vehicles. RISE invests in a test track where all sorts of traffic situations can be simulated.

In Italy, the Centro Ricerche FIAT (**CRF**) is set up in 1978. Some 800 technicians now work here full-time, spread across the entire country. Their research is divided into four categories: automation of the production process, the car and its bodywork, the power train and the materials lab.

FIAT subsidiary Comau focuses on the automation of the work process in the factory. The relationship between man and machine is central in their approach. In their philosophy, the approach of managers must change in the new working environment. To achieve this, a training scheme is introduced which is offered in collaboration with the French business school ESCP.

Poland has a rich manufacturing history. In the 1930s, Warsaw was the biggest aircraft manufacturer and exporter in the world.

The universities are still there, but the spirit of entrepreneurship was exiled when the countries became part of the Soviet Union.

A century ago, the Engineering Design Centre (**ECD**) had led the way in the aviation sector. Between the two World Wars, Poland had been a major exporter of planes, aircraft engines and helicopters. During the war, part of the facilities were destroyed (Daugherty, 2018), but the technological aviation knowledge was preserved after the war because the Communist government set up the General Institute of Aviation. Attempts to rebuild the factories failed; a lack of money and entrepreneurship meant the old glory days could not be brought back. Poland had lost its aviation industry.

After 1990, the American firm General Electric saw ECD's potential and was prepared to invest. Together with the General Institute of Aviation, GE gave a new lease of life to the ECD as a private-public institution. Today, some 1,800 engineers work there on making aircraft engines cleaner and more efficient with the help of 3D-printing. They do this in close cooperation with the local technical university and the GE engineers in Ohio.

In 2019, 35 knowledge institutions from 11 Polish cities set up the public Lukasiewicz Research Network. Research focusses on four areas: smart mobility, digital transformation, healthcare and sustainable economy and energy. At the request of a client, a team is put together in under a week from the more than 7,000 researchers who are part of the network. The customers are Polish companies and foreign firms with a branch in Poland. These include GE, Airbus and Philips Light as well as Poland's Pit Radwar, a specialist in radars, which is a subsidiary of the state defence company.

FRAUNHOFER: A FEDERAL APPROACH

How does a thoroughly German scientific institution get such a strong reputation in the USA? This was the question Antoine van Agtmael and I asked ourselves during our research for the book *The Smartest Places on Earth*. The Germans themselves say it comes from their 'Fraunhofer model.' Twenty-five years after its foundation in 1949, a committee decided that further expansion of the Fraunhofer Institute should be financed by the sale of its inventions. The reasoning behind this was that creating a more entrepreneurial spirit with the researchers could mean that they would connect more closely to the needs of industrial companies.

Another strength of the model is its federal infrastructure, which translates into 72 separate institutes, spread across the most populated country in Western Europe. Fraunhofer has test locations, often in cooperation with universities, where technologies like solar panels, cooling equipment, energy storage, fuel cells, electrolysis and new materials are studied.

Fraunhofer does not limit its collaboration to universities and large businesses with their own research facilities. To reach smaller and medium-sized companies, it works with 'provider of know-how and technology transfer' Steinbeis. This reach also extends to other countries: the Fieldlab 'For Artificial Intelligence and Digital Twins' aims to promote the digitalisation and the use of data by the SME sectors in the Netherlands and Germany.

Technical expertise embedded in Germany's DNA

Back in the 19th century, Ferdinand von Steinbeis was already convinced that technical vocational training could do with a helping hand. With his financial contribution, a network was created between the technical colleges in the federated state of Baden-Württemberg. Around 50 years ago, these vocational colleges set up a foundation called Steinbeis which used its technical knowledge to help small and medium-sized companies. The foundation grew rapidly and is now active throughout Germany.

FRAUNHOFER STIMULATES EUROPEAN COLLABORATION

It is a typically European phenomenon: institutes of applied science that support companies with the technological renewal of their machines. You can find these in countries with a strong industrial history such as Germany and Sweden. This European characteristic can also be seen in that the fact they are fragmented. Each institute has its own origins and specialisms. Even though working together may be not in their DNA, these institutions joined forces in EARTO in 1999, with the shared goal of increasing their visibility and 'voice' in Brussels. Later, Fraunhofer took the initiative to start organising substantive discussions via annual meetings.

Many institutions, even though historically focused on their own economy and companies, have a growing interest in what other institutions have to offer. They are encouraged in this by initiatives taken by the European Commission within the framework of the three transitions. For example, the creation of an International Dataspace by Fraunhofer is at the same time an invitation to other institutes to help develop a European platform which gives the control back to companies and government over the data they produce.

REFERENCES

Danish Technological Institute (2020) Building a Nordic innovation ecosystem around technology infrastructures and testbeds: A feasibility study of Nordic testbeds collaborations. Available at https://en.gts-net.dk/wp-content/uploads/2020/03/WP1-Building-a-Nordic-innovation-ecosystem_testbeds-Feasibility-study.pdf (Accessed 5 September 2023).

Daugherty, G. (2018) The city of engineers: How GE's technology center in Warsaw became a hub for engineers from around the world. Available at https://blog.geaerospace.com/technology/the-city-of-engineers-how-ges-technology-center-in-warsaw-became-a-hub-for-engineers/ (Accessed 5 September 2023).

Heide, M. de (2016) The financing of fieldlabs in the Netherlands. TNO report 2016 R11435. Available at https://publications.tno.nl/publication/34623736/CHnLkb/TNO-2016-R11435.pdf (Accessed 5 September 2023).

4

EUROPE'S BUDDING INNOVATION STRATEGY

Spring 2021. For the second year in a row, the Hannover trade fair is cancelled. Covid is the culprit that prevents industrialists, politicians and technicians from all over the world from physically meeting again. It does not prevent the CEOs of ASML, Carl Zeiss and Trumph from addressing policymakers in Brussels digitally. The European Commission is working on plans to have European chipmakers catch up to Asian and American producers. Is Europe going to achieve this by itself or do Intel, TSMC or Samsung need to assist? ASML, Zeiss and Trumph, makers of the most advanced smart chip machine in existence, are unanimous in their advice to the commission: don't go it alone but think in terms of a global ecosystem in which Europe already plays an important role. Let experienced makers of smart chips build a factory here, so the quality of the ecosystem will increase.

Twenty years ago, such a debate between companies and the EC on the latter's innovation policy would have been unimaginable. Policymakers and politicians in Europe were not attuned to the idea of innovation, nor to the ideas of establishing a common industrial policy. The market was just an area to be cordoned off, for companies to take on new challenges. And they did. But they soon found that the required technological

DOI: 10.4324/9781032703381-6

innovations were too complex to solve on their own. So ASML was looking for partners who would take care of part of the renewal. Only with the knowledge of Zeiss in the field of lenses and that of lasers at Trumph was ASML able to become a leader in the world with an ever smarter machine. An alliance was born that found its strength in sharing knowledge. The European Commission is now calling on companies, universities and regional authorities to also establish alliances to shape the necessary transitions.

FIRST STEPS

Why did it take so long for Brussels to develop its own vision of innovation policy? The answer is that policymakers have been followers, not initiators. The first seeds for what later became known as the EU innovation policy were planted in the mid-eighties. The ambition to create a single market for goods, people and services offered companies and universities an opportunity, but also posed a threat. The result was that they had to step out of their cocoon. To this end, they were enabled by a financial facility that Brussels set up during the same period for joint research by universities among themselves, or together with companies.

With a few billion euros, it was humble beginnings (see jeupiste.eu/horizon-2020-and-around/historical-timeline-framework-programme). Europe does not have a military-industrial complex like the USA does, which has been driving the need for technological research and innovation since the mid-fifties. In addition, the US DARPA has had a great influence through the deployment of research assignments at universities and companies. One of those assignments eventually led to the creation of the internet.

In the absence of a focused external stimulus, it is not surprising that the system that was set up in Europe had bureaucratic features. There was no defence or market push; the systematic organisation of the technologies to be investigated was leading. In addition, universities and companies from all member states had to be given the opportunity to participate in the studies.

THE SILICON VALLEY INCENTIVE

At the turn of the century, when European policymakers and politicians were beginning to wonder how their policies could spur innovation, ASML was looking for a working alliance model with its intelligent end users. At the same time, Philips decided to transform its closed research lab into an open campus. They too saw the need to forge alliances in order to be successful. Technology was becoming too complex for a single company to have all the relevant knowledge in-house. Very slowly, universities, most of which were still self-absorbed well into the Eighties of the last century, also discovered the need and usefulness of international cooperation.

But more was happening in the early 2000s. Entrepreneurs, politicians and researchers were discovering Silicon Valley. They saw how Stanford University commercialised its knowledge through startups, and how venture capitalists and other financers would discuss business plans with entrepreneurs at breakfast in roadside cafés. Many a visitor would leave with the feeling that anything would become possible.

Back in Europe, although the desire to embrace innovation, both technological and organizational, was strengthening, an established network of venture capitalist, start-up entrepreneurs and science institutes reaching out to each other was still missing. A world that could be seen, heard, experienced in California had yet to be built here.

NEW DYNAMICS

It would take about ten years for venture capitalists to discover Europe. They would quickly spread out from the financial heart of London, to Stockholm, Berlin, Paris and Amsterdam. Companies set up their own venture funds to keep an eye on upcoming start-ups that are usually located in the shadow of the ivory tower of the universities.

The universities, meanwhile, begin to commercialise their research. Departments are set up that specifically assist professors and students on their way to the market. So-called Incubators, organisations that aid the development of new business ventures especially by providing low-cost commercial space, management assistance or shared services become a breeding ground for talent. Private equity funds (usually set up within the many rich pension funds) enable startups to accelerate their growth. All these are grassroots developments; Brussels is standing by, searching for a role to play.

In 2009, the heads of government decided that Europe should stimulate a knowledge economy. They drew up a charter, but its text was still in stark contrast to what is already common practice in California. It would take a while before the bureaucratic layers were taken away from policy. The process was sped up in Brussels by taking advantage of the social upheaval caused by the financial crisis of 2007 and the disappointment felt when the proposed instigation of a European Constitution is voted out.

HORIZON 2020 AND BATTERY ALLIANCE

The European Commission wanted to get a clearer view on the available innovation capacity, so in 2014, under the promotional name of 'Horizon 2020,' bigger investments and simpler rules were promised. In addition to this funding instrument, the majority of which provided grants for a three- or four-year period, the commission set up the FET initiative, which stands for Future Emerging Technologies. According to the commission, this instrument was needed because many technologies and innovations require way more time and money for any individual company or research institution to come up with.

The first two 'Flagship' projects, Graphene (for use in inks, solar energy conversion and opto-electronics, among others) and the Human Brain Project (related to medical informatics, high-performance analysis and computing, and neuro-robotics, among others), received 1 billion euros for a period of ten years in 2010. In addition, other participants, like companies and local authorities, contributed to the research projects. Other projects included the Battery of the Future, ICT and the Connected Society, Environment and Climate change and others.

In 2015, the commission set up a 35 billion euro fund that should stimulate companies' investments by a total of 650 billion euros. Brussels saw a central role in this process for the European Investment Bank. The federal institute based in Luxembourg was to accelerate the companies investments with the help of new financial players such as private equity, corporate venture funds and the money of successful internet entrepreneurs. With the help of these new players and local authorities, and traditional investment banks, the initiative became a success.

Because of this, Horizon 2020 received a follow-up by Horizon Europe. This subsidy program has a span of seven years, from 2021 to 2027. A record budget of 95.5 billion euros is available.

But while the general programme of Horizon 2020 was still running, the European Commission also took the lead in defining the need for a specific innovation program. Noting that the automotive industry was quickly gearing towards electric transport, but that the batteries needed were almost all manufactured by Asian companies, Brussels called on entrepreneurs, local politicians and knowledge institutions to form alliances. This plan to create its own competitive and sustainable battery cell manufacturing value chain was dubbed the European Battery Alliance.

The European Investment Bank plays an important role in this ongoing alliance, providing start-up loans to new initiatives, such as NorthVolt in Sweden, which wants to make batteries for the automotive industry. When its new plant Nortvolt Ett will be opened in 2024, the EIB will be one of the first lenders. But a group of private Swedish investors, including Spotify founder Daniel EK, has also invested 600 million euros in the new company.

The commission reached a similar conclusion with regard to chip production. Its analysis shows that Europe depends on Asian and American producers for high-quality 'smart' chips. So EC drew up a plan that should lead to investments in the local production of smart chips. The question it presented to entrepreneurs and scientists: Should we develop this smart production ourselves or should we bring foreign companies from the USA, South Korea or Taiwan here? The answer was given when the Chips

Act came into being in 2022: Intel quickly announced a major investment in Magdeburg, with the company also opening production and research facilities in five other countries in Europe. TSMC followed in 2023 by announcing a factory would be built in Dresden with partners Bosch, NXP and Infineon.

With these initiatives, the European Commission has shown what its new role could be: identifying the weaknesses and undesirable dependencies that have arisen in European markets, and call on companies and knowledge institutions to pool their knowledge and commercial executive power. Another role that the commission has defined for itself is that of developer of quality standards, through new laws and regulations. In other words, it is building new markets in which quality and sustainability play a leading role.

5

EC 'CONDUCTING' THE EUROPEAN INDUSTRY

If the European Commission was slow to take on an active role in innovation processes, as outlined in the previous chapter, it was the Covid epidemic and the war in Ukraine that have really opened its eyes to the slowness, vulnerability and unwanted dependencies that have crept into our economy. Outsourcing of parts of the production process has ended up mainly in China, and it was assumed for too long that Russia would be a reliable supplier of gas and oil. A more balanced outsourcing of work and production – and even 'bringing home' crucial activities – has gained momentum. At the same time, a search for other reliable gas producers has begun.

The EC plays a central role in this. At the heart of its policy is the formation of alliances that share knowledge, so that new technological possibilities will increase European sovereignty. The EC has become a conductor, as it were, who has to persuade a group of idiosyncratic member states to form a balanced orchestra. A conductor cannot accept a false note, she is looking to bring out the virtuosity in everyone and bring these qualities into harmony with each other. She hands out the parts, sets the tempo and does all this working from a score. But should playing conditions change, she is capable of improvising.

DOI: 10.4324/9781032703381-7

The European industrial policy for the 21st century is such a score, a structure with which the energy and digital transitions must take shape. The backbone of this policy is the forging of alliances in which companies, knowledge institutions and local authorities share their knowledge. In terms of my previous book, written with Antoine van Agtmael, the ambition in Brussels is to make Europe a 'brainbelt.'

For that book, we visited American and European 'rustbelts' like Albany, Akron, Dresden and Eindhoven: regions in which an existential fear had taken hold after its defining industries had collapsed. This fear turned out to be the driving force behind a challenging vision that allowed them to come out of a deep rut. They turned from 'rustbelts' into 'brainbelts.'

In Europe, the fear of the depletion of the Earth was be taken to be that driving force. But, as urgent as that abstract ideal turned out to be, it was only from the moment the price explosion in the energy market became painfully visible to citizens and companies through exceptionally high bills, that the energy transition was seen and felt as a personal assignment.

PREVENTING A TECH SUPREMACY

Europe now feels that existential fear, and it must find its way in a world in which each power bloc with its own political-economic model strives to gain a dominant position with new technologies. China wants to be a technology leader by 2049. The USA wants to slow down that process by banning the supply of advanced chips, for instance. Washington hopes that its policies, supported by its partners in Asia and Europe, will keep China from gaining a leading technological position for a longer time.

The problem is that Western companies have not only discovered China as a place where production can be done cheaply. A growing group of companies now see China as a challenging market for their products. Many international chip companies have a production site in China, which puts them close to their customers, who are active in a wide range of industries, from automotive to medical applications. At the same time, those chips can be used to bring Chinese defence technology to a higher level.

Forming a united front requires all partners to have mutual trust and to avoid surprises. In August 2022, a sustainability agreement (the Inflation Reduction Act) was concluded in Washington by the US Congress. As a part of this, developing electric transport is encouraged, but under the condition that subsidies are only given to cars manufactured entirely in the USA. European, Japanese and Korean car manufacturers felt shut out by this, because the Asian battery manufacturers, in particular, produce important parts in their home markets. Although Europe is encouraging the creation of its own battery industry, it is up to the commission to give an appropriate response to nationalist measures like these.

The European Union's success in keeping the front united, even after the Russian army invaded Ukraine, is a thorn in the side of Russian nationalists. President Putin wants to restore Russia's old glory and pride and he sees the West (the USA and Europe) as a decadent obstruction. He would prefer to bring Europe back to its state in the 19th and 20th centuries; a patchwork of alliances that could easily be played off against each other.

The Sharing Brainpower initiative of the European Commission also wants to promote alliances, not between countries but between companies, universities and local authorities. This initiative has the potential power to increase connectivity and cooperation.

WELL FUNDED TO STIMULATE TRANSITIONS

The commission has a unique instrument at its disposal. Within the framework of the Corona Recovery Fund, it can raise hundreds of billions by issuing Eurobonds. Member states can receive grants and loans if they submit a plan that focuses on sustainability and digital transitions. The commission also reviews what structural improvements can be made to the applicant and whether the rule of law and freedom of expression are not compromised. The first plans were submitted in mid-2021.

In addition to the Recovery Fund, the commission has drawn up a Green Deal within the framework of the regular budget, which is intended to stimulate sustainability. More than 1,000 billion euros have been allocated for this for a period of ten years.

The commission has taken steps to tackle a number of existing dependencies. During the Corona pandemic, the EC took care of the joint purchase of vaccines. And in 2023, it took care of the purchase of more than 30% of the required natural gas. In this way, the purchasing power of the Union was effectively used with the aim of security of supply at the lowest possible price.

ACTION FROM BELOW, CONTROL FROM ABOVE

The commission does not just need to identify gaps and potentially harmful dependencies. Sharing-brainpower initiatives also come to life when member states express a clear ambition to say goodbye to fossil fuels and switch to sustainable energy sources. In February 2011, the Danish government announced its 'Energy Strategy 2050,' with the stated aim to be fully independent of fossil fuels by 2050. It was the starting signal for the profitable generation of wind energy on the North Sea. The success is such that the EC was able to join in with the Danish plan to convert the generated electricity into hydrogen via electrolysis.

Another initiative that the commission was able to support came from Germany. German politicians, entrepreneurs and scientists had been discussing the consequences of digitalisation of society in the context of Industry 4.0 for a decade. One of the key questions was how data created on software from different suppliers could be shared without these suppliers somehow limiting or making use of the information flow. The myriad small and medium-sized enterprises in Germany, specifically, did not want to get caught in the grip of some large domestic or foreign tech company.

The federal government therefore proposed to create a sovereign digital space in which companies or institutions remain owners of their data. Fraunhofer carried out the assignment and developed an International Data Space (IDS). The member states and the commission have seized on this development and are now also calling for the creation of a European Cloud. Germany has taken the lead in drawing up a common standard with other industrialised countries, so that data can also be exchanged globally on equal terms. Europe is even working to create a Public Goods function in addition to the commercial function of data companies.

EUROPE SHOULD STAY ITS COURSE

Russia and China are each fighting in their own way to become global leaders. They both draw on a rich past and consider it fair that their opinion should be heard and that other countries take note. Any criticism is disrespectful.

Europe rejects this culture. To stay afloat in these new global relations, Brussels chooses to promote 'unity in diversity.' Sharing Brainpower is a technical and cultural challenge that must be – and in many instances already is – deeply rooted in our society and economy. Bringing scientists, technicians, entrepreneurs, and politicians together should not become an empty slogan, left to linger in boardrooms or parliaments. It is an effective instrument in a multipolar world in which flexibility in collaboration with new, trusted partners in Asia, the Middle East and Africa will be needed.

PART II

THE ENERGY TRANSITION

6

HOW EUROPE FOSTERS SUSTAINABLE ENTERPRISE

THE GREEN DEAL

In November 2016, glasses were raised in Paris when an agreement was reached to reduce CO_2 emissions to zero by 2050. But the big question was, of course, how would that ambitious goal be achieved? That evening there was widespread joy among activists, governments and companies. But as is so often the case, the next day the atmosphere was decidedly more sober. Companies were willing to endorse the goal, but felt that government should take the lead; activists were convinced that investors and financiers should immediately stop putting their money in oil and coal.

Did the name-calling start here? A stalemate was to be expected, but did not come. The European Commission picked up the gauntlet and formulated the Green Deal, in which it indicated the intermediate steps to be taken on that long road to 2050. It was not a multiannual plan, but a call to member states and companies alike, to determine the rate at which CO_2 emissions should be reduced. Very deliberately, an 'intermediate goal' was formulated: a 40% reduction by 2030, later increased to 55%.

The European Commission hereby created a strong top-down signal to the member states to tackle the energy transition; it

DOI: 10.4324/9781032703381-9

would later do the same with regard to the European protection of data traffic and digital personal data.

In the Green Deal, the EC coordinates the consultations between the member states and the European Parliament that should lead to the legal framework within which industrial sectors should achieve emission reductions. The Polluter Pays principle is leading, so businesses and consumers are presented with the bill. For emissions, companies must buy certificates that are gradually becoming more rare, so that their price will increase. But that should not be at the expense of the competitiveness of companies, so a CO_2 limit tax was introduced that will tax the import of fertiliser, cement, steel, iron, aluminium, electricity and hydrogen. This should compensate European companies for the higher costs.

With the new legal framework, companies and individuals are encouraged to adapt their behaviour and opt for sustainability. In this way, local processes towards the innovative resurrection of old industrial regions, in which Sharing Brainpower played and still plays a crucial role, are now aided by legislative incentives from the commission.

GERMANY'S SECOND 'ENERGIEWENDE'

Europe's largest economy is an indispensable link in the energy transition envisioned by the European Commission. Germany has always been at the forefront of energy policy in Europe. This dates back to the 1970s, but the first 'Energiewende' that the country is known for came into being in March 2011, shortly after the disaster with the Japanese nuclear power plant in Fukushima. The German cabinet decided to close its own nuclear power plants for the long term. Gas was seen as the least polluting fuel. Within the framework of EU policy, in which trade is the desired means of stabilising relations with Russia, in particular, two pipelines were built under the Baltic Sea, Nordstream 1 and 2.

In 2022, a significant external shock gave European energy transition an unexpected boost. In response to the war in Ukraine, Russia was renounced as a supplier of relatively cheap gas. New suppliers of (liquefied) gas were sought, energy saving was high on the agenda and the search for sustainable energy sources such as sun, wind and hydrogen received an unprecedented push. It accelerated both top-down (national, EU) and bottom-up initiatives (from knowledge centres and the business community).

For Germany, this Second 'Energiewende' is a new focus on the energy transition. The Scholz government can partly build on the work of its predecessor. In the last year of her reign, Chancellor Merkel set up a few plans for developing a hydrogen strategy. Nine billion euros have been set aside for the construction of a hydrogen infrastructure. By 2030, 5 gigawatts of hydrogen will be produced, and double that by 2040.

These plans are the result of 'bottom-up' pressure from the industry. The steel industry and the chemical industry made it clear that only with a new raw material – hydrogen – will they be able to achieve the sustainability of their companies. Siemens, producing windmills and marketing its own *electrolyser* that can convert electricity into hydrogen, has been an early supporter of stimulating this new sustainable raw material for the basic industry.

Berlin has set up a foundation to get the production of the expensive hydrogen up and running. The first, H2Global, has launched in 2021. The foundation organises two separate auctions: one with producers and one with buyers. The cheapest offering producer and the highest bidding customer are selected. The foundation will pay the difference between the two prices at the auction. The German Ministry of Economics has made 900 million euros available.

More than 50 companies and institutions have already registered with the foundation. The Dutch government has pledged allegiance to the foundation because it wants to continue to maintain a prime role of Rotterdam, which has traditionally been the transit port for oil and coal to German industry, also for hydrogen.

EFFECTS OF THE SECOND 'ENERGIEWENDE'

It's not surprising that Germany is formulating clear guiding lines but also responding adequately to the wishes of the industry. The tide is high. Wind energy and hydrogen must play a key role in the energy transition. Terminals must be built along the coast of the North Sea and Baltic Sea in which the liquefied natural gas can be stored.

In Berlin, the civil service is in execution mode. The government took over the direction of the regions, which led to a significant acceleration in the construction of gas terminals. In addition, the storage terminals will receive a dual use function. In the long term, these plants can also be used to store hydrogen.

In parallel, the Fraunhofer Institute in Dresden is working on the development of a membrane that enables the simultaneous use of hydrogen and natural gas in the gas network already operational in Germany and the Netherlands. The membrane separates the two fluids.

In the short term, the 'heightened state of alert' in Germany has aligned a number of stakeholders in the energy sector and a financing mechanism has been set up to start the production of hydrogen. Energy producer RWE and steel company Thyssen Krupp and Shell, together with BASF, have ambitious plans for the construction of wind farms in the North Sea, experimenting with the creation of hydrogen at sea.

COMMERCIAL SUCCESS IS PROOF OF THE PUDDING

The proponents of hydrogen point to the progress made over the past decade in making offshore wind farms profitable. At first, producers had to be enticed with subsidies to build a park. Nowadays, larger, more efficient windmills have made the parks profitable, eliminating the need for subsidies.

The key to this success lies in Denmark, where parliament opted for renewable energy from wind and sun early on. Energy company Ørsted used this support to achieve commercial success. But Ørsted also understood the power of Sharing Brainpower: the company started a process with its chain of suppliers, bundling knowledge and innovative strengths. In the next chapter, I outline how the North Sea has continued to be a source of energy, first through oil and gas, and now through wind energy.

7

WIND BLOWS LIFE INTO THE ENERGY TRANSITION

TWO SIMULTANEOUS TRANSITIONS

In September 2018, I was in Copenhagen at the annual meeting of my former colleagues from the European Business Press. As is the custom, a company visit was part of the programme. This year, we visited the Danish energy conglomerate Ørsted. CEO Henrik Poulsen told us passionately about the transformation to sustainable energy.[1] When Poulsen started at Ørsted, the company was still owned by the state and most of the electricity was generated from fossil fuels. He sketched the scepticism he received from foreign politicians when he talked about his plans. Investors and analysts were also hesitant, until 2013, when Goldman Sachs was allowed to play a vital role in the financial transformation.

Poulsen was in essence trying to realise two transitions simultaneously: To turn a state-owned company into a listed company whilst delivering on its promise to divest of all fossil fuel activities; and to break away from fossil fuels to focus completely on sustainably generated energy, with offshore wind in the lead role.

Poulsen showed with a simple calculation that this switch can only succeed if the productivity of offshore wind turbines goes up. He went on to explain how Ørsted saw the need to form

DOI: 10.4324/9781032703381-10

an ecosystem with suppliers, other energy companies, universities and knowledge institutes. For innovations to grow quickly and effectively, the company's management talked to its suppliers at an early stage. Ørsted told them that this was a challenge that could only be met if they worked together.

A HISTORY OF BRAIN SHARING

Innovation and sharing knowledge are not new to the company. In 2008, when it was still state-run DONG (Danish Oil and Natural Gas), Ørsted was already active with other energy companies in the Offshore Wind Accelerator (OWA). The spiritual father of this initiative is Britain's Carbon Trust, which from the beginning of this century has committed itself to providing an insight into combined CO_2 emissions and developed standards which companies can use to measure the reduction of emissions (Carbon Trust, 2018).

The concept of the Offshore Wind Accelerator is simple. Participating companies discuss improvements that can be made to the wind platform. During their joint research, each turbine remains under the control of its energy producer, but all knowledge regarding cables, foundations, geoscientific knowledge of the sea floor et cetera is shared and added to.

Bottlenecks are translated into projects which third parties can sign up to. Equipment to provide a better 3D image of the sea floor, the development of a manoeuvrable ship which can approach wind parks more safely, strengthening the foundations (necessary when rotor blades become bigger and the wind park is located further offshore), the doubling of voltage to 66Kv to make cabling more efficient are just some of the 150 projects that the group has implemented together in the last ten years, which have led to significant cost savings. In that decade, the OWA has expanded from five to eleven companies, including Scottish, Norwegian and German energy producers. Shell was the last company to join OWA.[2]

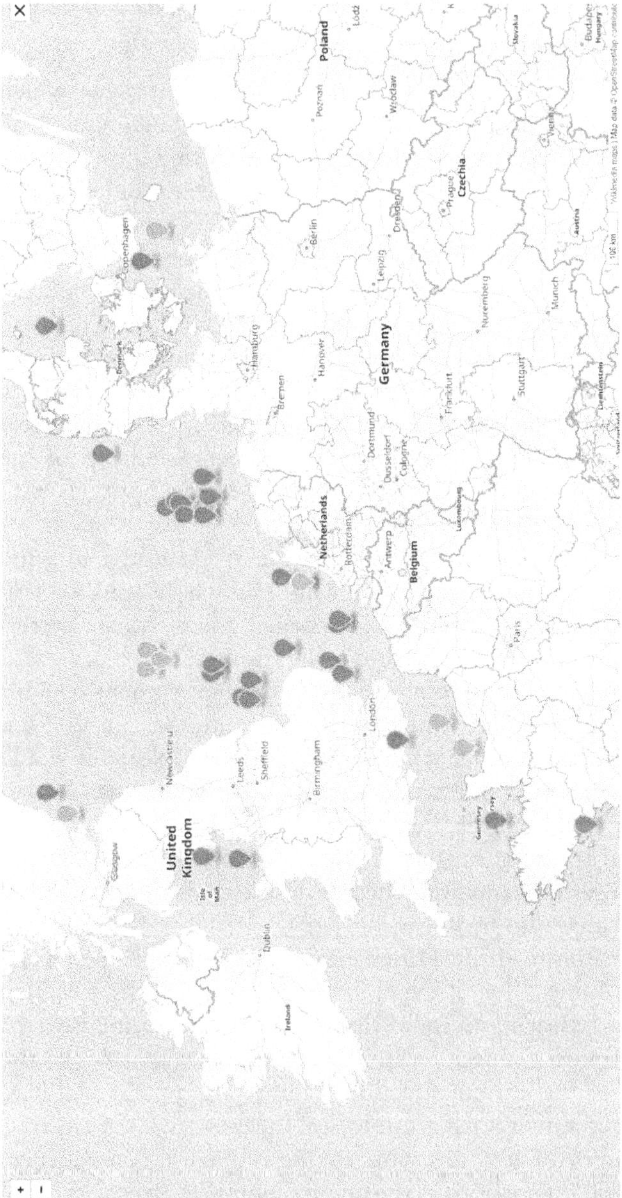

Figure 7.1 Operational (dark) and proposed (light) offshore wind farms in Europe.

Source: Wikipedia, October 2023. "List of offshore wind farms", map available at: https://en.wikipedia.org/wiki/List_of_offshore_wind_farms#/map/0.

VISION AND VITALITY KEEP THE DANISH WIND SECTOR FOCUSED

The OWA receives support from the Danish government, which issues the wind park concessions. The government requires all those involved to share knowledge acquired during the construction of the wind parks with the rest of the sector and with the scientific world.

In the past few decades, Denmark has been a prime example of a successful 'top-down' energy transition plan. The country's politicians had decreed early on that, in line with the European Green Deal, the use of fossil fuels should be completely replaced by sustainable energy sources in 2050. The most important of these would be wind energy. The combination of this clear long-term goal with the courage and entrepreneurship of the Ørsted management is the foundation of Denmark's success with wind energy (Johansen, 2021).

In the process, Ørsted has become the world leader in wind energy, the costs of constructing wind parks have sunk so that government subsidies are no longer needed, and the total electricity yield from wind parks has improved strongly.

But Denmark keeps going. In 2010, the government decided that it would build a wind park in the Baltic Sea. In 2020, it decided to build another wind park in the North Sea; this would add to international endeavours because other wind parks further out to sea could deliver their electricity yield to it before being transported to shore. Further, Denmark is in talks with international energy companies on whether the electricity generated can be transformed into hydrogen.

The dynamism of the Danes means that they and their partners are gaining a lot of experience with wind parks. Location is important. Bearing in mind that the EC wants to increase the total wind power capacity to 150 GW in 2040 (a factor-10 rise compared to the current situation),[3] future wind parks will have to be located much further out to sea. But how will the electricity be transported to shore, what are the ecological consequences and how will fluctuations in the energy supply be dealt with? And should tenders for new parks still be coordinated by national governments? These technological, environmental and organisational advances require that many of the decisions to be made move up from the Danish level to a European level.

How does wind electricity reach the shore?

Most of the wind parks from the last decades are situated close to the shore (to about 30 km). National grid operators have installed fixed 'power sockets' in the sea and these are linked to the national energy grids. If the distance from the shore is more than 80 km, more expansive cabling has to be laid. But future wind parks will need to be even further out to sea. Tennet, Dutch Gasunie, the Port of Rotterdam and the Danish grid operator Energinet have done a study into other solutions, such as aggregating the supply of various wind parks on a new location. This could take the shape of an artificial island or a floating platform (North Sea Windpower Hub, 2019).

EUROPEAN COOPERATION AND PROMOTION OF WIND PARKS

The European Commission recognises that driving up the total capacity of wind energy production can only be achieved if countries and existing wind parks work together. Because each country has its own legal framework, the EC has agreed at ministerial level that they will first focus on three projects in countries whose frameworks are closely aligned (European Commission, 2022). In the first project, for instance, Belgium, the UK and the Netherlands are working together. The grids of the last two countries are already connected to each other.

A bigger challenge is expected at Dogger Bank, about 100 km off the east coast of England. The potential is enormous: 70 to 100 GW, but the complexity, both in technical and legal terms, is also huge. This point in the North Sea has the advantage of being relatively shallow and having stronger winds than elsewhere. But the distance from shore is so great that it will be necessary to work with collection point (the so-called hub-and-spoke model).

From a legal viewpoint, five countries aim to work together on the Dogger Bank: the UK, Norway, the Netherlands, Denmark and Germany. They must all complete their own legalities and allocate concessions. Brussels has indicated that it will be of prime importance to harmonise their regulations.

GERMAN BIGHT: AN EXAMPLE OF BOTTOM-UP INNOVATION

With Denmark and the transition to wind power, we have seen how the initiative to renew was initiated and furthered by a strong vision from the national government. But in the German Bight (the south-eastern section of the North Sea), it is industry giant Shell that takes the lead. In February 2020, together with Gasunie and Groningen Seaports, the company presented a plan to build an enormous wind park with a capacity to produce 3 to 4 GW of electricity for hydrogen production in 2030. Germany's RWE and the Norwegian Equinor have joined the consortium.

Their shared goal is to create a hydrogen factory in the northern Dutch port of Eemshaven (more on this in the next chapter) which can deliver 800,000 tons of hydrogen to industrial clients in the Netherlands and north-west Europe via Gasunie's pipeline network. The electricity generated can be transported via a cable which connects the Dutch and Danish networks and comes ashore at the Eemshaven. Hydrogen production on location at the wind park is also viewed as a possibility; the necessary gas can be delivered via existing networks.

Although initiated bottom-up, Shell is asking the national governments for subsidies. Ørsted did the same, and since the plans fall within the European Green Deal and the Danish vision to have the industry be working completely on renewable fuels by 2050, chances of financial backing are very likely.

WHERE TO STORE ALL THE ENERGY?

With the production of offshore wind energy against increasingly lower costs and the ambition to generate more capacity even further out at sea, the question arises where surplus wind energy can be stored. What was only whispered five years ago is now being said out loud: hydrogen can play that role. There are still technical limitations which make the production of so-called 'green hydrogen' uncompetitive. But according to scientists, industry entrepreneurs and energy companies, if we can temporarily bridge the gap with subsidies, we can create a head start and make Europe the global leader in the hydrogen economy.

The European Commission also sees the potential for hydrogen; in its Green Deal, an important role is reserved for this new primary raw material. With EC vice-chairman Frans Timmermans presiding, the first discussions took place in late 2020, with representatives from industry, entrepreneurs, universities, start-ups and others who were asked to form alliances.

In the next chapter, taking hydrogen as a lead, I will describe how the commission brings its industrial policy into practice, where ecosystems are created and what the role of the 'Electrolyser' is.

NOTES

1 Poulsen resigned as CEO on December 31, 2020 at his own request and became a member of Ørsted's supervisory board. He also joined A.P. Moller Holding, to which the shipping company Maersk also belongs, as an adviser. He is a member of A.P. Moller's investment committee).

2 Ørsted has also built a network of Scandinavian, British and American universities and knowledge institutes such as Fraunhofer and the Energy Research Center of the Netherlands (ECN, now part of TNO). See also Holm, 2018.

3 1 GW is enough to power around 750,000 homes straight from the source, but with transmission leakage it will realistically be enough for about 300,000 homes (Source: US Dept of Energy and others).

REFERENCES

Carbon Trust (2018) 10 years of accelerating innovation: A summary of the impact of the Offshore Wind Accelerator. Available at https://www.carbon-trust.com/news-and-events/insights/10-years-of-accelerating-innovation (Accessed 5 September 2023).

European Commission (2022) The North Seas energy cooperation. Available at https://energy.ec.europa.eu/topics/infrastructure/high-level-groups/north-seas-energy-cooperation_en (Accessed 5 September 2023).

Holm, J.S. (2018) Ørsted wind power way of working with RD&D. Available at https://www.sintef.no/globalassets/project/eera-deepwind-2018/presentations/opening_holm.pdf (Accessed 5 September 2023).

Johansen, K. (2021) Blowing in the wind: A brief history of wind energy and wind power technologies in Denmark. *Energy Policy*, Vol. 152, May 2021, 112139. doi: 10.1016/j.enpol.2021.112139

North Sea Windpower Hub (2019) Modular Hub-and-Spoke: Specific solution options. Available at https://northseawindpowerhub.eu/files/media/document/Concept_Paper_3-Specific-solution-options.pdf (Accessed 5 September 2023).

8

EU TAKES LEAD IN BECOMING THE FIRST HYDROGEN ECONOMY

The success of wind energy is an important boost to energy transition in itself. But it can also speed up another transition: the green transition in the steel and chemistry sectors, which must lead to the structural reduction of CO_2 emissions. Converting renewably generated electricity into green hydrogen can provide European industry with a new raw material. Additionally, hydrogen can be used to make mobility more sustainable. And finally, hydrogen can be used as a sort of storage battery to dampen the peaks and troughs of the frenzied surplus-and-shortage cycle of sustainable electricity.

The European hydrogen market is currently being built up at great speed. The EU is taking the lead, but advocates that it should involve business from step one. In the summer of 2020, the European Commission called on businesses, with industrial giants Shell and Siemens in the lead, to enter into alliances in the hydrogen chain. The commission has drawn up legislation to organise a European gas market. Since the summer of 2022, hydrogen has been awarded the status of 'Important Project of Common European Interest'; this IPCEI measure gives greater leniency to state support.

DOI: 10.4324/9781032703381-11

Hydrogen primer

The production of hydrogen plays a key role in any industrialised society, since hydrogen is required for many essential chemical processes such as oil refining and the production of ammonia and methanol.

As of 2022, 96% of European hydrogen is produced with natural gas, resulting in carbon dioxide emissions. This is often referred to as 'grey hydrogen' when emissions are released to the atmosphere, and 'blue hydrogen' when emissions are captured through carbon capture and storage (CCS). Blue hydrogen has been estimated in the USA to have a carbon footprint 20% greater than burning gas or coal for heat.

Renewable hydrogen can be obtained via electrolysis using renewable electricity to split water into hydrogen and oxygen. It can play a key role in decarbonising sectors where other alternatives might be unfeasible or more expensive. It can be used to replace fossil-based hydrogen for transport and industrial processes and to start new industrial products, such as green fertilisers and steel.

When produced at times when solar and wind energy resources are abundantly available, renewable hydrogen can also support the EU's electricity sector, particularly its power grids, providing long-term and large-scale storage.

Sources: 'Hydrogen' at Wikipedia and European Commission, 2022a.

Germany, the biggest early adopter, has already set up a foundation, H2Global, which will organise separate auctions of hydrogen supply and demand. The German government has allocated 900 million euros to bridge the price difference between demands and offers.

Top-down initiatives such as the aforementioned IPCEI and the European Clean Hydrogen Alliance work best with a visible pioneer, respected by all parties, a *Connector*. In the EC, it was the Dutchman Frans Timmermans; his experience in languages, diplomacy and international relations made him very suitable for this task. He set up an advisory board in which entrepreneurs, scientists and representatives of local organisations take place; more than 600 have already done so. In addition, a commission has been established that will define the major investment projects, map the obstacles and stimulate the ecosystem between regional administrators, research institutions and companies.

The European Clean Hydrogen Alliance was given a challenging goal by Timmermans: In 2030, 40 GW of hydrogen should be produced via electrolysis, a process whereby water is split into oxygen and hydrogen. The challenge is not a judicial nor an organisational one, but a technical one. The bottleneck is the capacity of electrolysis cells, which at present is a maximum of 20 MW. This means that with the current state of technology, many so-called *electrolysers* have to be coupled together. This places high demands on, for example, the foundations of hydrogen plants, especially in the water-rich, swampy areas of Northwestern Europe.

SHELL AND SIEMENS PICKING UP THE GAUNTLET

Shell and Siemens are both advocates for the large-scale development of green hydrogen. Shell already uses hydrogen as a diluter in the refining of crude oil; the company is the first to use sustainable hydrogen generated via electrolysis as an energy source at its German refinery.

Under its own NortH2 plan with the Dutch province of Groningen, Shell wants to build an electrolysis installation at Eemshaven, which should deliver 4 GW of hydrogen in 2030. The electricity will come from a wind park that still has to be constructed in the North Sea. Further scaling up to 10 GW in 2040 is projected. This equates to 0.4 million tonnes of green hydrogen in 2030 and 1 million tonnes of green hydrogen by 2040 – enough to compensate a full year of traffic emissions in Norway.

In another project, Shell wants to produce 200 MW of hydrogen on the Rotterdam Maasvlakte; wind energy is the source for the electrolysis process. Shell is also working in Rotterdam on a 'blue hydrogen' project with BP, ExxonMobil, Uniper and Gasunie, converting gasses from their combined oil refineries into hydrogen. (Blue hydrogen is the product of grey hydrogen production in combination with CO_2 capture and storage. As such it is an alternative to green hydrogen.) The Dutch government supports the project with a subsidy of 2 billion euros.

Siemens specialises in the electrification, automation and digitalisation of both primary and secondary industry, with a special focus on software development (Industry, Energy and IT Solutions are three of its six main parts.) The company has already built up a strong position in the hydrogen chain. Its wind turbines play a prominent role in the offshore wind market, and its electrolysers convert renewable electricity into hydrogen. In conjunction with German railways, Siemens is working on a hydrogen-driven train and with the Fraunhofer Institute, it is researching how to improve hydrogen production.

To ensure a good political connection with EC regulators and policymakers, it made perfect sense for these two companies to appoint Ben van Beurden, former CEO of Shell, and Joe Kaeser, CEO of Siemens at the time, to the advisory board set up by Frans Timmermans. A good top-down Connector can function best if he or she is part of a team of bottom-up Connectors (European Commission, 2022b).

SIEMENS REACHES OUT TO CONNECT

Because it is an electronics company at heart, Siemens has to rely on intensive cooperation with other parties. Decades ago, the company was looking for a position in Denmark for the development and production of wind turbines. Spain's Gamesa became its permanent partner.

With its *Silyzer*, Siemens introduced an electrolyser that can produce hydrogen with, for example, wind power. Siemens and Gamesa obviously worked together to further this product, but still reached out to other third parties. For example, in Denmark it worked together with start-up Green Hydrogen Systems (FuelCellsWorks, 2020). This company uses an alkaline electrolyser (see Box) which converts water into hydrogen with a 3 MW wind turbine. The hydrogen can then be delivered to buses, taxis and cars as fuel.

In the autumn of 2019, Siemens opened a joint hydrogen knowledge centre with Fraunhofer in Goerlitz, on the border with Poland. An innovation campus for high-tech companies has also been set up on Siemens' industrial terrain. The company initially put 35 million euros into the project.

Two techniques

There are currently two major electrolysis techniques. One involves the use of an alkaline solvent. According to a study by TNO and FME (FME/TNO, 2020), alkaline systems have been used on a large scale for years, primarily for the production of chlorine. The more recent technology (polymer-electrolyte membrane, PEM) is generally more efficient and more flexible, but currently has a maximum capacity of around 20 MW.

A NEW MARKET, MULTIPLE KEY PLAYERS

What the experience of Siemens shows is that, in an emerging market around emerging technologies, cooperation is vital. For Siemens, it was a simple necessity because of its focus on electronics. But with the hot breath of European Commission standards and goals in their neck, it is only to be expected that multiple key players are eager to add their contributions. Given the technological challenges, producers of electrolysers such as Norway's NEL ASA and Britain's ITM Power play a particularly vital role.

Shell has worked with ITM Power for some time. In 2018, they built a 10 MW electrolyser at the Shell refinery in Germany. It is still the biggest industrial application, with a peak capacity of 1,300 tonnes of hydrogen per year. This project is supported by Brussels to ensure that knowledge and experience can be shared in the European hydrogen chain. Other participants in this project are Norway's Sintef, specialised energy consultancy Element Energy, and Sphere, a software developer which focuses on industry.

An electrolyser for the home environment

When Sebastian-Justus Schmidt, owner of a software development company wants to build a sustainable house in northern Thailand in 2011, he is looking for a business that can supply an electrolyser. However, the firm he chooses soon goes bankrupt and Schmidt decides to take it over himself. He regards his electrolyser as an energy storage facility with which decentralised power generation can be further professionalised.

He sets to work in Thailand with his first product. He takes an apartment complex off the local electricity grid; wind and sun generate more than enough electricity. The surplus is converted to hydrogen via electrolysers. If wind and sun are unavailable, a fuel cell can convert the hydrogen into electricity.

In 2017, Schmidt sets up his company Enapter (https://www.enapter.com/use-cases/residential-multi-home-phi-suea-house). With the experience gained in Thailand, the business case for Enapter takes form. The company's ambition is to make it possible for everyone to produce hydrogen in their own house. As a storage capacity, but also to use as fuel for the car. In this way, whole new energy systems can be created locally. People and companies in remote areas and on islands can also generate and store their own electricity.

ITM, by the way, is making a lot of headway in (PEM) electrolyser technology advancement. Both at home in Sheffield and in Germany, working with Linde, the company keeps raising the bar in the volume and capacity of its electrolyser units. Linde became a shareholder in ITM, and they set up a joint venture that's led from their office in Dresden.

Norway's NEL ASA is the oldest electrolyser producer. The company built the world's first electrolyser with alkaline technology over a century ago. Since the 1950s, it also gained experience with PEM technology. With the takeover of an American company in 2017, NEL ASA is currently world leader in the PEM technology. It shares its knowledge with Shell and is a research partner in a project financed by the American government. Other current projects are located in Denmark and France.

A FLURRY OF ACTIVITY

Now that people finally embrace the fact that wind and sun can generate large – but fluctuating – amounts of electricity, there is a worldwide search for the right storage capacity. There are two obvious routes to thinking about this: hydrogen, or batteries.

Thomas Edison already experimented with nickel-iron batteries, but produced unreliable results. Still, Fokko Mulder, Dutch professor of Energy Storage and student Bernhard Weniger at the Technical University of Delft, consider the nickel-iron battery a brilliantly simple idea. In 2016, they built a small battery which, when charged, automatically starts to produce hydrogen (TU Delft, 2022). In this way, they produce hydrogen with a total efficiency of 90%. They also do not need to use any rare raw materials; nickel and iron are cheap and available everywhere.

The *Battolyser*, as it is called, functions well in the lab – but will it also perform in an industrial environment? Swedish utility provider Vattenfall and Dutch engineering company Proton Ventures have already expressed interest in the technology; and with the support of the Wadden Fund, a Battolyser the size of a sea container is now operational at the Eemshaven (Crolius, 2018). The quality of the hydrogen is being tested, after which scaling up to a capacity of 10 MW is the next step.

At companies and research institutes big and small, and with the funding and active cooperation of the European Commission, the search for the affordable production of hydrogen, the new gold, is in full swing. There is a flurry of activity in many connected fields. But as we saw earlier, the basic industry also needs to explore other avenues to achieve the 2030 emissions target. Harnessing and storing wind and solar energy is only one part of the equation.

REFERENCES

Crolius, S.H. (2018) Battolyser attracts grant funding, corporate support. Available at https://www.ammoniaenergy.org/articles/battolyser-attracts-grant-funding-corporate-support/ (Accessed 5 September 2023).

European Commission (2022a) Hydrogen. Available at https://energy.ec.europa.eu/topics/energy-systems-integration/hydrogen_en (Accessed 5 September 2023).

European Commission (2022b) Key actions of the EU Hydrogen Strategy. Available at https://energy.ec.europa.eu/topics/energy-systems-integration/hydrogen/key-actions-eu-hydrogen-strategy_en (Accessed 5 September 2023).

FME/TNO (2020) Electrolysers: opportunities for the Dutch manufacturing industry. Available at https://www.fme.nl/system/files/publicaties/2020-11/FME-TNO-Summary%20report%20electrolyser%20production%20NL.pdf (Accessed 5 September 2023).

FuelCellsWorks (2020) Siemens Gamesa Chooses Green Hydrogen Systems (GHS) as Electrolysis Partner. Available at https://fuelcellsworks.com/news/siemens-gamesa-chooses-green-hydrogen-systems-ghs-as-electrolysis-partner/ (Accessed 5 September 2023).

TU Delft (2022) Battolyser Systems. Available at https://www.tudelft.nl/innovatie-impact/innovation-projects/projects-2022/battolyser-systems (Accessed 5 September 2023).

9

BATTERY CHAIN

THE PUSH AND PULL OF MARKET FORCES

EC INITIATES ITS LARGEST BRAIN SHARING INITIATIVE

The development of the electric car has advanced immeasurably in the last 20 years, since Tesla set the standard in 2008. With some European car manufacturers eager to make the switch, and many countries and cities planning to ban the sales of internal combustion engines by 2035, the European Commission has backed this business-driven development, but has strengthened the initiative by focusing on the construction of a completely new European battery chain.

In its analysis of the situation, the commission states that the natural consequence of the introduction of electric cars – a growing demand for batteries – will lead to an undesirable dependence on Asian suppliers, in particular. Research of the commission shows that some 85% of all batteries are produced in Asia, with the EU contributing a meagre 3%. Japan and South Korea were top producers for a long time, but meanwhile, China is now the world's leading battery supplier (60%).

The 2017 initiative of the European Commission to set up its own battery chain provides insight into how different member states react to this top-down step. The Swedish government opted out; it had already focused its national research on electric and safe mobility and was ahead on a slightly different path. France, as well as Germany, countered the initiative with an appeal to the

DOI: 10.4324/9781032703381-12

commission for enlarging state aid. But Berlin also started to invest in its own industry research into the Battery of the Future. Poland, one of the countries in which many non-European automakers have taken up residency in recent decades, is joining the alliance. In the Netherlands, which does not participate, the initiative was a booster for research into a 'forgotten' invention that charges batteries faster and provides more capacity.

Under the acronym EBA – European Battery Alliance – entrepreneurs, researchers, local politicians, start-ups and financiers were invited to share knowledge, start co-creations and co-invest. The whole chain – research, raw materials, suppliers, producers, clients and recycling – has to be built from the ground up. The commission's ambition is to accelerate the EU towards a leading position on the battery market by developing a legal standard for the whole chain, with special focus on sustainability, re-use and recycling, as well as clean and safe production. EU batteries should be of high quality, produced with the help of smart software and should be rechargeable and be able to return excess power to the network.

The initiative raises the question of what role the Asian producers would play. Should they be included in the European think tanks and research groups looking for the Battery of the Future? Another worry was the availability of the necessary raw materials: lithium, nickel, cobalt, manganese and graphite. These raw materials come from Australia, Congo, Chile, Indonesia, Canada and China. The commission wants to safeguard Europe's position on these markets via regular trading discussions (European Commission, 2020). At the same time, the search for lithium in Europa has intensified. In Sweden, France, Spain, Germany and in the Czech Republic large stocks have been found.

THE EBA NETWORK

The commission has set itself the task of developing a standard to which all European and non-European suppliers should adhere. The commission has been given the green light by the European Parliament for legislation to regulate recycling over the next decade. Legislation must now be integrated into the member states. Seven countries – Sweden, Poland, France, Germany, Italy, Finland and Belgium – are part of the European Battery Alliance, which in a short period has attracted over 500 industrial companies, startups and knowledge institutions.

The EBA network is coordinated by EIT InnoEnergy. This equivalent to America's Massachusetts Institute of Technology was set up at the beginning of the 21st century. José Barroso, president of the European Commission at the time, wanted to locate this institute in Lisbon. But because it was deemed to become too expensive and would represent unfair competition to other universities, the network was deployed as a virtual institute, organised around different themes.

At the end of 2019, after intensive lobbying by Paris and Berlin, the European Commission gave the Battery Alliance the status of Important Project of Common European Interest, meaning the seven contributing countries can each provide state aid separately but still work together across their borders. Within one year, 3.2 billion euros in state aid was approved. In the period 2020–2030, Brussels will add some 10 billion euros in aid.

To coordinate work within the EBA more efficiently, four working groups will be set up in which 17 companies and knowledge institutions will be able to cover the complete chain. With all of the above, the first steps have been taken to build the necessary alliances and ecosystems in which local governments, knowledge institutions, companies, start-ups and vocational training schools can find each other.

SWEDEN: EXPERIENCE, DEEP POCKETS AND A SUPPORTIVE GOVERNMENT

In a way, Sweden was well prepared for the European Commission's top-down initiative to build a European battery chain. In 2017, the Swedish government promised 100 million euros for a research laboratory that Chalmers University had established in Gothenburg with knowledge institute RISE. The Swedish Electronic Transport Laboratory (SEEL), as it is called, focuses on multidisciplinary research to study the many aspects of the electrification of transport. Scania, Volvo Group (Trucks), Volvo Cars and her Chinese mother-company CEVT (China Euro Vehicle Technology) are working together here.

In Sweden, government traditionally plays an important role 'from the wings' when it comes to building ecosystems. It moves to bring together parties after companies and organisations themselves already have made the first decisions and selections. Consolidating the wide range of research institutions in RISE and locating its headquarters near the Chalmers University in Gothenburg is an example of this. A separate research project concerning recycling was initiated with metal company Stena, which has become a leading party in the processing of and trading in scrap.

Swedish battery producer Northvolt has joined both the EBA and the recycling research project. Much of Northvolts focus and dedication is due to CEO Peter Carlsson who, after a long career with Ericsson, NXP and Tesla, returned to Sweden in 2015. In interviews, Carlsson stated that he wants to prove that Europe is able to build its own megafactory by building one in Sweden (Mathis & Nauclér, 2022).

He certainly has been capable of bringing in funds: in 2018, Carlsson's company Northvolt received 52 million euros from the European Investment Bank to set up a facility in Västerås, about 80 km west of Stockholm, to do research into battery cells. This facility also houses a demonstration production line. Three years later, Northvolt set up a factory in Skelleftea, in the north of Sweden, which can produce batteries for 750,000 electric cars annually. According to Carlsson, 25 of these factories are needed to meet the 'explosive' European demand in the coming decades.

BMW and Volkswagen quickly signed up. BMW placed an order of 2 billion euros in batteries to be delivered in 2024; Volkswagen has invested 900 million euros in a second Northvolt factory to be built in Salzgitter, Germany. According to Carlsson, these car manufacturers are keen to see a battery factory in their 'backyard' because co-creation between Northvolt and the car designers is absolutely vital. After all, the size of a battery is a crucial factor in any electric car design (Hueck, 2019). Add to this a second EIB loan of 350 million euros and the 600 million that a group of Swedish investors under the leadership of Spotify CEO Daniel Ek had brought together, and it is evident that Northvolt is a serious force in Europe, with a capital of almost 3 billion euros.

The plans for building a second plant in Germany came in jeopardy when Carlsson hinted in interviews at opening a plant in the USA instead, following Joe Biden's promise of billions of dollars in subsidies to attract foreign companies that will help stimulate the North American energy transition. In reaction to this protective move, the European Commission further lifted some of the limits to state support, opening the door for the Germans to compensate for the amount of subsidies a European company would get in the USA.

THE FRENCH–GERMAN TANGO

After the launch of the EBA in 2017, Germany and France were quick to start several national initiatives, while lobbying the EC for regulations and funds enabling them to work both nationally and internationally. Little wonder, then, that French and German politicians were keen to announce their plans to cooperate. France's finance minister Bruno Le Maire and his German colleague Peter Altmaier announced a joint investment of 5 billion euros in 2019.

Their national initiatives are in close conjunction with (and usually located at the plants of) national car makers like PSA (Peugeot, Citroen, Opel) and Daimler. In 2021, this company merged with FCA from Italy (Fiat, Chrysler), opening up the cooperation even further. Other participants are battery maker Saft (a subsidiary of Total Energies) in France. Two battery factories will be built; the first to the south of Lille, at a Peugeot manufacturing site. The second factory will be built in Kaiserslautern, Germany, on an Opel site.

But apart from the joint operation with France, Berlin is also supporting the research in the Battery of the Future in its own federalist way: 1 billion euros went to research institutes in North

Rhine Westphalia to merge their research into the battery of the Future under the name MEET. The German government and two federal states also invested 300 million euros in established battery producer Varta. This investment will give Varta, expert in small, household batteries, the opportunity to test its newest compact technology for use in larger batteries, including car batteries.

Meanwhile, Fraunhofer has given focus to its 20-year knowledge base on batteries in its own Fraunhofer Battery Alliance.

ASIAN BATTERY PRESENCE IN EUROPE

For some time, Germany has been a favourite home-away-from-home to non-European battery producers. China's CATL, for example, built its first international factory in Erfurt, so that clients like Volkswagen, BMW, Daimler, Volvo and Bosch could be served better and quicker. CATL has publicly spoken of its desire to carry out joint research with its clients but also with knowledge institutions such as MEET (Waldersee, 2023). Another Chinese company, SVolt, is building a 24 GW-capacity factory on the German-French border in Saarlouis, to provide battery packages for 300,000 to 500,000 cars a year. A third Chinese party, Farasis Energy, has located a factory producing battery cells north of Leipzig. Daimler has a strategic cooperation with this company (Mercedes-Benz, 2020). Farasis also has R&D facilities in Stuttgart.

China has decided to gradually divest of cheap mass production and focus on world leadership in the field of research and innovation. Higher domestic consumption and more added value from high-quality technological products are motivating factors. From this perspective, it is understandable that China is eager to open research and production facilities in Europe.

Poland is also host to a few of Asian battery producers. The country has a rich tradition in aviation R&D and still has a large number of engineers carrying out applied scientific research. The Asian companies are mainly located in the south-western part of Poland around Wroclaw, and receive assistance from a keen government. In this way, a Polish ecosystem is gaining shape.

Korean LG Chem, specifically, chose the Europe route and decided to expand its production capacity to Poland. Starting in 2018, its European production capacity will be increased to 65–70 GW, with a total investment of 2.8 billion euros. After investigation, the EU approved the financial support from the Polish government as falling within its legal agreements. The LG factory will now be the biggest in Europe, producing enough batteries for one million cars annually. The Belgian 'materials technology and recycling group' Umicore will be an important supplier of the cathodes (nickel, manganese, cobalt) used in the batteries. The two companies are in talks on a contract in which Umicore will be responsible for the recycling of old batteries.[1]

As a final example, BYD, a Chinese battery and car manufacturer from Shenzhen, has entered the market for temporary electricity storage, together with Poland's solar panel producer ML Systems. They produce big batteries, placed in containers, used to cope with the large fluctuations in the production or industrial use of electricity. A second Chinese company has established a factory in Wroclaw to produce the chemical raw materials for the battery producers.

IN SEARCH OF THE 'BATTERY OF THE FUTURE'

Worldwide, universities, research institutes and start-ups are researching solutions to improve car batteries: accelerate charging, increase safety, increase the distance covered, from the current 500–700 km to at least double that.

The search for the 'Battery of the Future' is taking place in various places in Europe. Fraunhofer has taken the lead in Munster together with MEET, and in Gothenburg science and business have found each other in the SEEL initiative. In Belgium and France, chemical company Solvay and France's SAFT are building a European ecosystem. Siemens and Manz, a German specialist in battery cell parts, have joined this initiative.

In Eindhoven, start-up SALD entered the market with a coating developed by TNO and Fraunhofer. This coating can be used in the current liquid variant of a Li-Ion battery. This already provides a number of advantages: a car battery can be charged to 80% capacity in just 10 minutes; in another 10, it is fully charged. Also, a car with this sort of battery can travel between 1,000 and 2,000 km.

Volkswagen has set its sights on the American start-up QuantumScape which produces a solid-state battery.

The advantages of this type of battery are a rapid charging time and a very long lifespan: 80% of the capacity is still available after it has been charged 800 times. Together with VW, QuantumScape wants to set up a pilot line in Salzgitter to build batteries for between 10,000 and 20,000 cars annually.

ECOSYSTEMS AROUND RECYCLING

An enormous amount of used car batteries is to be expected between 2025 and 2030. In Gothenburg, Northvolt is working with the local university and a number of companies on a sustainable and effective way to recover raw materials from the used batteries. But research is also going on elsewhere to make energy transition circular by giving 100% of the used materials a new life.

A major player on the recycling market is the aforementioned Umicore. This Belgian company uses a technology which heats empty batteries to an extremely high temperature so that raw materials can be retrieved from the residue. Umicore processes 7,000 kg of batteries annually in Antwerp.

But scientists are coming up with new technologies that do not need high-temperature incineration, which is currently the norm in recycling. Obviously, the recycling process itself should also be as energy-efficient as possible. Research has been carried out at the University of Braunschweig, Germany, and in Nivala, Finland. This method, which is still in development, already makes it possible to recycle 91% of materials used.

A MIX OF BOTTOM-UP INITIATIVES AND EU DIRECTION

Looking back on the last four chapters, we can see that the urgency in the energy transition came when companies and individuals were required to pay the price of gas supplies from Russia being cut. Germany and other countries dived headway into the search for energy savings and new gas suppliers; they also increased the use of renewable energy, such as solar and wind. Denmark took an early lead in the field of wind energy through the explicit policy of successive cabinets that want to say goodbye to fossil energy sources in the 2030s.

Under pressure from many basic industry players, the European Commission proposed to set up a sustainable hydrogen alliance that will build the entire chain from scratch. The commission did the same when it became aware that the European car industry was massively opting for electric mobility. The European Battery Alliance was set up.

NOTE

1 Umicore itself situated in Nysa, south of Wroclaw, where a cathode production line will be established with the help of an EIB loan of 125 million euros. Umicore is strengthening its link with the region by working together with the local technical college to provide research and education on sustainable mobility. A test laboratory with the most modern equipment – including a 3D-printer, lasers, drones and a robot – will make it possible for students and Umicore technicians to discover new working methods together. The initiative exudes the spirit of the Fieldlabs in Eindhoven and Drachten.

REFERENCES

European Commission (2020) Critical raw materials resilience: Charting a path towards greater security and sustainability. Available at https://eur-lex.europa.eu/legal-content/EN/TXT/?uri=CELEX:52020DC0474 (Accessed 5 September 2023).

Hueck, H. (2019) Hoe Northvolt de slag om de batterij wil winnen *(in Dutch)*. Available (through log-in) at https://fd.nl/weekend/1359080/hoe-northvolt-de-slag-om-de-batterij-wil-winnen (Accessed 5 September 2023).

Mathis, R.W., Nauclér, T. (2022) Giga-scaling low-carbon batteries: A chat with Northvolt CEO Peter Carlsson. Available at https://www.mckinsey.com/capabilities/sustainability/our-insights/giga-scaling-low-carbon-batteries-a-chat-with-northvolt-ceo-peter-carlsson (Accessed 5 September 2023).

Mercedes-Benz (2020) Strategic partnership with Farasis. Available at https://group.mercedes-benz.com/innovation/drive-systems/electric/mercedes-benz-and-farasis.html (Accessed 5 September 2023).

Waldersee, V. (2023) Politics aside, China's CATL ramps up cell production in Germany. Available at https://www.reuters.com/technology/chinas-catl-german-plant-targets-six-battery-cell-production-lines-by-end-2023-2023-01-26/ (Accessed 5 September 2023).

PART III

THE CO_2 AND SUSTAINABILITY TRANSITIONS

10

CAPTURE AND STORAGE OF CO_2

COMMITMENT IS KEY

Europe remains and will remain dependent on energy imports. The energy transition, necessary as it is, will not change that. Brussels is now fully committed to the production of green hydrogen, but even if the targets are met, the import of gas and green or blue hydrogen remains necessary. In addition to investing in sustainability, oil companies will have to look at gas exploration and extraction. This is also necessary because Africa and Asia, whilst becoming more affluent, will increase their energy consumption.

The transition to sustainable fuels, at whatever speed, remains a process of paradoxes. Saying goodbye to Russian gas, for example, meant that Germany had to go back to using more lignite to generate electricity. Another paradox is the European Commission's decision to approve and support the 'temporary' storage of CO_2 in empty gas fields under the North Sea. The industry has indicated that this underground storage is a vital step to reach the increased target of CO_2 reduction in 2030. Opponents of subsidising CO_2 storage fear postponement of the necessary adjustments by the industry.

For the European Commission, however, Carbon Capture and Storage (CCS) is the right temporary instrument to achieve a minimum reduction of 55% CO_2 by 2030. For the Norwegian government, capturing CO_2 and storing it under the North Sea has long been an integral part of its policy for sustainability.

DOI: 10.4324/9781032703381-14

Gas-fired power plants and the capture of CO_2 go hand in hand there. And just like in Denmark, where an unwavering political vision led to a flourishing wind economy, in Norway an ecosystem has been created around the storage of CO_2.

NORWAY: EARLY ADOPTER OF CO_2 STORAGE

The Norwegian government was an early supporter of capturing CO_2 and storing it in empty oil fields under the North Sea at the end of the last century. Norwegian state oil and gas company Equinor built up experience, together with research institute Sintef and Aker, a specialist in CO_2 capture.

For Norway to commit to the Paris Agreement, the government decided to promote CCS on a large scale. In several industrial processes, such as cement production, CCS is necessary to significantly reduce emissions. In their 'Longship' policy plan, the government pledges to help strengthen Norwegian industry by enabling businesses to meet the climate requirements of the future (Norwegian Government, 2021). Thus, the project is an important contribution to green growth and will secure and create new jobs in the industry.

In addition, 'Longship' facilitates the production of blue hydrogen from natural gas in combination with carbon capture and storage. Hydrogen is highlighted in the European Green Deal; production of blue hydrogen is seen to have great potential for value creation in Norway and for cutting greenhouse gas emissions in Europe.

In 2012, the Norwegian government set up a research institute in Mongstad, north of Bergen, which focuses on CCS. Norse energy company Equinor is running the Mongstad Technology Centre (TCM). Afterwards, Shell and TotalEnergies (France) joined as co-owners of the initiative. A test installation was built in a fjord to try out new and cheaper forms of CO_2 capture.

Equinor has been pumping 1 million tonnes of CO_2 captured from gas-fired power plants a year into the Sleipner West gas field since 1996. Part of the 'Longship' plan is the intention to make the storage in empty gas fields commercially viable. Oslo has invested over 2.5 billion euro into this venture. The government expects other countries and the EU will support the project financially.

In 2021, Equinor, Shell and TotalEnergies set up a new joint venture to transport and store more CO_2 in the former Norwegian gas fields: the Northern Lights project. The aim is to process between 3.5 and 5 million tonnes of CO_2 annually. All European companies can deliver their CO_2 here. To make the project a success, a pipeline is laid to south Norway that gives Ireland, Britain, Belgium, the Netherlands, France and Germany the opportunity to deliver the CO_2 in liquid form. The delivery can also be made by ship. Final preparations on the necessary infrastructure in the port of Oygarden are taking place.

Table 10.1 Greenhouse gas emissions, worldwide

Greenhouse gas emissions, worldwide *(2021, gigatonne fossil CO_2)*	
China	12.5
United States	5
Europe	3
India	2.9
Russia	2

Source: JRC report (2019).

Table 10.2 Greenhouse gas emissions, Europe

Greenhouse gas emissions, Europe *(2021, kilotonne CO_2-equivalent)*	
Germany	760
UK	429
France	420
Italy	417
Poland	399
Spain	289
the Netherlands	167

Source: UNFCCC.

Table 10.3 Greenhouse gas emissions, Europe, per sector

Greenhouse gas emissions, Europe, per sector *(in 2021)*	
Energy supply	26
Domestic transport	23
Industry	22
Residential and commercial	13
Agriculture	11

Source: European Environmental Agency.

WHO PAYS THE FERRYMAN?

Equinor has positioned itself as the pivotal point for the underground storage of CO_2 in the Scandinavian region. Shell is preparing to take up a similar position in the Rhine-Scheldt delta. Refineries, chemical plants, steel factories and fertiliser producers are well represented in Flanders and Zeeland, in Rotterdam and Moerdijk and in Limburg and the German Ruhr area. These companies have an enormous demand for the capture and collective storage of CO_2. The cement industry alone, much of it positioned along the Rhine river, is responsible for 7% of worldwide CO_2 emissions.[1]

In Germany, CO_2 emissions are Europe's highest, but the country's population is also the most averse to underground storage. On-shore storage is completely off the agenda, so then-chancellor Angela Merkel suggested focusing discussions on the possibility of using empty gas fields under the North Sea. Would German industry become a client, the business case for the ports of Rotterdam and Eemshaven would see profit more quickly.

CO_2 EMISSIONS AND AGRICULTURE

Today's intensive agriculture and livestock farming threatens biodiversity and depletes the soil on which work is carried out. By 2050, food production with minimal fertiliser and pesticide use should be standard, bio-dynamics and circularity should be the norm, not the exception, and remuneration to the farmers should be reasonable. In addition, this sustainable form of agriculture should restore biodiversity.

These are huge tasks because European agricultural policy has been a combination of regional policy and the promotion of intensive agriculture and livestock farming since the 1950s. Sicco Mansholt, then-Eurocommissioner of Agriculture boosted this policy in the 1970s, reasoning that the famine at the end of the Second World War (mainly affecting the Netherlands) was no longer allowed to occur; Europe had to guard itself against any future shortages. This policy led to larger farms and further mechanisation.

Sustainable agricultural policy must put an end to maximimalist, soil-depleting production. The European Parliament voiced its disappointed in 2020 when the multiannual EU budget, which runs until 2027, was presented but, to their mind, did not display a necessary reallocation of funds within the agricultural policy.

Some member states, with France at the forefront, see the current agricultural policy as a means of maintaining the quality of life in its regions. Europe is experiencing an aging population and a migration to the city; in rural areas, such migration is leaving its traces far and wide. Shops are closing their doors, doctors and dentists are difficult to find or their practices extend over large areas, children have to be taken to schools far away, public transport is severely reduced and social activities are only organised sporadically.

An economic revenue model in which profitability is key can only lead to social decline. From this perspective, sustainability also deserves the necessary attention and financial resources.

NOTE

1 PBL Netherlands Environmental Assessment Agency has calculated the cost price for the capture of CO_2. Factors such as density and the extent to which the CO_2 is polluted are important here. For Dutch refineries, the cost price comes out at around 80 euros per tonne. If the actual price via the Emission Trade System (ETS) is lower, companies would have to pay the difference. The Dutch government has decided to pay the difference in price until 2030. Some 2.5 million tonnes will have to be captured annually.

Shell will be responsible for half of this number, which is around a quarter of the refinery's emissions. If innovations reduce the cost price or the price of emission rights rises, the subsidy will be decreased accordingly.

REFERENCE

Norwegian Government: Ministry of Petroleum and Energy (2021) Questions and answers about the longship project. Available at https://www.regjeringen.no/en/topics/energy/landingssider/ny-side/sporsmal-og-svar-om-langskip-prosjektet/id2863902/ (Accessed 5 September 2023).

11

A PATCHWORK APPROACH TO THE CIRCULAR CHEMICAL INDUSTRY

NEED FOR CLEAR DIRECTIVES

In its Green Deal, the European Commission has not only set a carbon-neutral target for 2050 and the reduction of CO_2 emissions to zero. It also fosters the creation of a Circular Economy within 30 years. Parts of this goal include sustainable consumption and growth, prevention of waste and keeping resources used in the EU as long as possible. The chemical, construction and agricultural industries play crucial roles in achieving this goal.

The chemical industry is willing to reduce CO_2 emissions via the capture of CO_2 and the development of green hydrogen well into the next decade. But how are participants going to make their industry circular? Companies and researchers have asked their governments for help. Not principally in the form of financial support, although this does come into play, but mainly in terms of measures which will gradually influence their processes and products to become circular.

With both the digital transition and large parts of the energy transition, it has proven to be best if the EU provides goal-setting policies. The setting up of the International Data Space (IDS), the battery chains and the hydrogen alliances are examples of

DOI: 10.4324/9781032703381-15

this. In the Green Deal, the European Commission has set up the Emission Trading System to control CO_2 emissions, making the polluter pay for the emissions it produces. This clear directive is a helpful tool for chemical companies reduce their CO_2 emissions, but is not enough to achieve a circular business operation.

Until the EC's Circular Economy Plan of 2020, there have been no guiding policies to influence either companies or consumers. Without a clear policy – whether restricting or directive – active participants were left to their own devices. This has resulted in a wide range of spontaneous activities, all playing a small part in the transition towards a circular chemical industry. These activities fall into four main categories:

1. *CO_2 as energy source in chemical processes*: In Germany, for example, an alliance between Siemens and the chemical company Evonik is taking steps towards the electrification of the petrochemical industry. It is carrying out a study into the feasibility of converting CO_2 into green chemical products via electrolysis and biotechnology. The German government stresses the importance of this project by investing 3.5 million euros.
2. *Research into organic, sustainable raw materials*: In France, Global Bioenergies, together with L'Oréal and the sugar company Cristal Union, is looking for a way to produce isobutene – an important, non-pollutant chemical compound used for making plastics, refrigerants and aerosols. The Netherlands' Corbion and Germany's BASF are studying the possibilities of green amber for comparable purposes.
3. *Recycling*: In the Netherlands, Sabic is working on improving the recycling of plastic. Dutch chemical company DSM wants to re-use its strong plastic yarns. They are bringing in the vision and energy of startup companies.
4. *Combinations*: Major projects in the Netherlands are working on solutions to make the chemical industry circular in the longer term. In one of these, a group of Dutch universities, applied science colleges, research institute TNO and

companies such as Shell, Dow Chemical and Avantium are working on the electrification of the chemical industry. At the same time, companies, universities and farming organisations in the southern Netherlands are joining forces so that the chemical and agriculture will be linked more closely together. The initiative is directed from the industrial complex Chemelot; sawdust and sugar beet are expected to deliver the main sustainable raw materials. Chemelot is also developing recycling initiatives.[1]

A one-man Brainpower project

Not only big companies and start-ups are developing these sorts of bottom-up initiatives. In the Netherlands, Johan Sanders, a retired professor from the University of Wageningen, is working on a new product which will ensure a more efficient use of grass, which could result in cows emitting 30% less nitrogen.

In his professional career, Sanders had already grappled with the question of how to use grass more efficiently. Only cows have stomachs which can process grass. In his own company Sanovations, Sanders worked on a solution (See grassa.nl/en/products/). He found one in the form of a machine that crushes and squeezes the grass so that the juice and the fibres are separated. The fibres are fed to cows as roughage which still contains 50% of the grass' proteins. This is sufficient for the cow to produce milk, but its digestion results in 30% less nitrogen emissions. Once they have been heated, filtered and dried, the proteins that remain in the juice are suitable for use in chicken or pig feed, as a replacement for soy imported from Latin America.

E-REFINERY: MAKING CO_2 THE NEW FUEL

A unique ecosystem is set up under the leadership of the Technical University of Delft (TU Delft). Around 40 researchers from seven universities and four applied science colleges have thrown themselves into constructing a so-called 'e-refinery,' focusing research 'on the electrochemical conversion of sustainable electricity, water and air into fuels and chemical building blocks, from the molecular scale to large-scale system integration.' The project was set up by Paulien Herder, professor of energy systems at TU Delft. The initiative for this brain sharing project came from the Dutch Research Council (NWO). The many institutions involved in the project bring a lot of different disciplines to the project.

The starting point was to make CO_2 the new, sustainably produced raw material for the chemical industry. The goal is to build large-scale storage systems for sustainably generated electricity. Researchers have three technologies in mind for this: the production of hydrogen, the production of hydrocarbon from CO_2 and the so-called redox flow-batteries (TU Delft, 2020; see box).

Redox flow-batteries

Redox flow-batteries were developed by NASA around 50 years ago and then ended up in a forgotten corner after the rise of the lithium-ion battery. The redox flow-battery is safer because it uses non-flammable fluids, and storage capacity can be expanded.

But the redox is too expensive; therefore, the efficiency must be increased and the costs reduced. In Eindhoven, the university and the national energy research institute DIFFER, together with MIT in the USA, have found ways to increase the efficiency. In the meantime, Fraunhofer has come up with a new way to reduce costs by 40%.

In the Dutch project, the electrolyser again plays a pivotal role. There is work being done on the design of an industrial-scale electrolysis factory, in which TNO is also taking part. They are thinking of scaling up the electro-conversion to gigawatt level, which would mean a thousand times more production than under the current systems.

In the meantime, TNO has picked five locations in the Netherlands where such a large facility could be set up. The cost and size (and the demands made on its foundations) will be partly determined by the tempo in which the electrolyser can be scaled up, and what consequences the new technology will have for the weight of the equipment.

AMBITIOUS GOALS

In consultation with industry leaders, it has been agreed that TU Delft's e-refinery will start production of three much-used raw materials: the bulk chemicals hydrogen, formic acid and ethylene. After this, the electrochemical production of other materials will be looked at. The government and Shell have invested 5 million euros, and a large number of companies have joined the project, including TATA Steel, Gasunie, Ørsted and Dow Chemical (TU Delft, 2019).

Both the goals and the planning of the project are extremely ambitious. Scientific breakthroughs are needed in many areas and these must be tested in trials and prototypes before they can be introduced at an industrial scale. As a rule of thumb Shell, which has considerable experience with carrying out complex research projects, works on the assumption that it takes between 20 and 30 years to go from idea to operational implementation. Professor Herder was aware of the complexity and the time pressure: 'There is little time for testing and scaling up because if transition needs to be ready in 2050, the new chemical industry will have to be built between 2030 and 2040.'

BIOREFINERY: AGRICULTURE AND CHEMICAL INDUSTRY JOIN FORCES

For decades, agriculture and the chemical industry have operated independently, so that two separate chains have existed alongside each other. The chemical industry works with fossil raw materials, with supply and price determined on the international markets. After refining, fossil raw materials deliver rich sustenance for the chemical sector, out of which a wide range of polymers can be obtained. For the chemical industry, every new raw material guarantees supply reliability and transparency around price forming.

The market for arable and livestock farmers is decided by interference from the government in the form of income guarantees, quotas or subsidies. The farmers' organic raw materials (sugar beet, for example) are tied to the season and their price and usability value are extremely dependent on all sorts of factors that cannot be easily influenced. No new raw materials are to be expected.

What can bring these industries together? That is the question chemical parks in the Dutch regions of Zeeland, West-Brabant and Zuid-Limburg decided to answer. These 'knowledge regions' have already asked Arnold Stokking to help them. At the end of the 1990s, Stokking was involved in the introduction of open innovation at Philips, which required a lot of 'feeling one's way' through the many possible connections and routes forward. Later, he and his TNO colleagues set up the Fieldlab concept, and he was also responsible for the building of ecosystems around photonics. In 2019, he became director of the Brightsite Centre at Chemelot, Geleen.[2]

At Chemelot, Stokking is responsible for pushing forward the Green Chemistry New Economy programme. In West-Brabant, the centre of Dutch sugar beet cultivation, an ecosystem has emerged with Dutch 'plant-based cooperative' Royal Cosun, Saudi chemical concern Sabic and OCI Nitrogen as the main players. The latter two companies are also involved in Chemelot.

Stokking has made his task even more complicated by adding the high-tech sector in close-by Eindhoven to the mix. But once there, Stokking was just a short train ride away from Terneuzen, where Dow Chemical and Yara (the latter already prominent at Chemelot) are active. It turned out to be easy to join some more dots. In Terneuzen, residual heat is exchanged. Dow Chemical receives waste gasses from steel producer ArcelorMittal in Ghent, and, in turn, delivers hydrogen to Yara for the production of fertiliser.

Experience the biorefinery in Ghent and Delft

In 2010, professor of Bioscience Engineering Wim Soetaert built a biorefinery environment in Ghent. With state-of-the-art instruments, he offers start-ups and established companies a place to experience what the newest biochemical processes can offer. His modest stated goal is 'to have them leave smarter than when they came in.' This is the same reason DSM, Corbion and TU Delft started the Bioprocess Pilot Facility (BPF) on the BioTech Campus in Delft in 2012. The goal of the BPF is to give start-ups and companies in the food and chemical industry the chance to work with the latest fermentation technologies.

Chemical industry leaders, meanwhile, aren't riddled with the choice for either electrification of processes (and building an e-refinery) or a transition towards biomass as a raw material (and building a biorefinery). Their main concern is how to refurbish or connect their existing installations to any new technology, and what adaptations are needed during the transition. For their money, either option must offer a reliable supply of new raw materials and transparent pricing.

Plasma technology: a CO_2 alternative

Plasma is the fourth state of matter: the other three being solid, fluid and gas. In a plasma reactor, a process is initiated by which methane (as natural gas) is converted into hydrogen and ethane without the need to burn the natural gas – which means that no CO_2 is emitted. Ethane is the basic raw material in the production of plastics.

Gerard van Rooy, who was appointed professor of Plasma Chemistry at the University of Maastricht in 2020, is doing research into first-generation technology and, together with Sabic and OCI Nitrogen, is considering the business case. When this research is done, they will assess how a second-generation reactor can improve efficiency and further reduce electricity consumption. The second-generation plasma reactor is due to be operational as a demo installation in 2025. It must be able to produce 12 tonnes of hydrogen.

Plasma reactors can also be an ideal solution for farmers in developing countries, since sunlight, water and air are the ingredients that a plasma reactor can convert into fluid manure. Professor Fausto Gallucci of the Technical University Eindhoven believes a small plasma reactor can be ready for market soon (Renewable Carbon News, 2021).

FINDING SUSTAINABLE RAW MATERIALS

In Bergen op Zoom, West-Brabant, research is done into using sugar as a sustainable raw material for the chemical industry. In 2014, Dutch Rabobank (traditionally strongly invested in agriculture) and the Biobased Industries Consortium asked Deloitte consultants to carry out a feasibility study into biomass as a basic raw material for the chemical sector. Sugar beet came out as the most promising candidate (Vaessen, 2016).

An important finding was that sugar beet cultivation in Germany, Flanders and the Netherlands is efficient; the distance between farmer and factory is short and, by further breeding of the seeds, can match competitors in Brazil, South-east Asia and the USA in terms of price and quality on the global market. The liberalisation of sugar beet cultivation, introduced by the European Commission in 2017, further strengthens Europe's position.

Deloitte's advice was clear and concise: build a biorefinery which can process sugar beet. Use this to gain experience and simultaneously focus research on improving the refining of sawdust (lignin – see box below), a second source which could be used by the chemical industry as a basic raw material.

But will the chemical industry invest hundreds of millions in a biorefinery that will process sugar beet? According to chemical industry veteran Willem Sederel, they will never do so (Sederel, 2019). With 40 years of experience in the chemical sector at General Electric and Sabic, Sederel claims the sector has a 'mortal fear of volatility and wants security of supply above everything else.' And betting on just one horse is also totally out of the question, he says. This is the reason he is also, like Deloitte, looking at lignin as a second raw material.

Lignin as replacement for oil

In 2015, the first step was made to combine biomedical knowledge from Maastricht with technical know-how from Eindhoven. On the initiative of DSM, TU Eindhoven, the University of Maastricht, the Academic Hospital in Maastricht and the province of Limburg, InScite, the Institute for Science and Technology was created. This is a place where bio-medics, bio-engineers and company researchers can meet. The institute has its own laboratories and services so that it can set up pilot projects.

An example of such a pilot is a process by which lignin, a class of complex biopolymers found in wood, can be converted into an oil that can serve as fuel or a raw material. The paper industry extracts lignin from wood pulp, in the process of making paper white. For them, lignin is just a waste product to be incinerated, even if it can amount up to 30% of materials used. But it is exceptionally suited for converting into raw material for the chemical industry.

The initiators of the InScite pilot are Michael Boot and Panos Kouris. They have developed their own patented process through which biomass can be cut up in an easier way. At the end of this process a fluid called 'Goldilocks' remains, from which an oil can be made (See: vertoro.com/technology). They tested and refined this process in the pilot facility at InSciTe; they have also set up a start-up. A demo facility will be built in Örnsköldsvik, on the east coast of Sweden (Sekab, 2020). It will initially produce lignin oil to replace the extremely polluting heavy fuel oil used in shipping.

CONNECTING INNOVATORS WITH COMPANIES AND FINANCIERS

Willem Sederel is not just a critic, he is also a Connector. Sederel began his career with Shell Research in Amsterdam and spent 26 years with General Electric, which culminated in the position of Chief Technology Officer of Polycarbonate for GE Plastics. When Sabic acquired GE Plastics in 2007, he maintained global leadership of polycarbonate technology for two more years and then became Global Innovation Leader.

In 2013, shortly before his retirement but still working for Sabic, the Saudi chemical producer welcomed the Green Chemistry Campus on its grounds in Bergen op Zoom in the Netherlands.

Sederel saw potential in advancing a biobased circular economy and became chairman of the Circular Biobased Delta at the Campus. This triple-helix organisation aims to accelerate the raw material transition by biobased routes and circular solutions. It quickly became a magnet for all sorts of circular initiatives.

Sabic buys adopts a sharing culture

Founded in 1979, Saudi company Sabic has now joined the ranks of the world's largest chemical concerns through takeovers in Europe. But with the takeover of the base chemical operations of DSM in 2002 and the chemical activities of General Electric five years later, the company also took over a culture of cooperation. DSM is the architect behind the Chemelot campus, home of the biorefinery, where its researchers also work. Although it does not have its own research in Europe, Sabic effortlessly shares the Limburgers' ambitions. In nearby Bergen op Zoom, the company is open to Sederel's initiative to set up a campus on its own grounds to attract outside knowledge.

In 2019, the Green Protein Excellence Center was opened at the Campus. This separate initiative was set up by Cosun, university of applied science HAS in Den Bosch and fermentation startup The Protein Brewery. These three decided to make it their mission to develop the Center into an incubator for start-ups and SMEs from the southern Dutch region of Brabant. The initiators want to make sustainable protein from residual green energy. Cosun is going to make sustainable protein from the leaves of sugar beet. The Protein Brewery has developed its own method for getting protein from potatoes, sugar beet and corn. Founder Wim de Laat has already raised 22 million euros from financiers to produce proteins on an industrial scale.

CIRCULARITY AND PLASTIC RECYCLING

In Europe, some 27 million tonnes of plastic waste is produced. About 25% of that amount is landfilled, and an equal amount is incinerated. Nearly one-third is mechanically recycled. This recycling process is expensive because the plastic has to be sorted into colour and type. Also, the EU exports a lot if its waste (plastic and otherwise) to other countries for treatment; a politically touchy, and costly, process. Add to that the damage being done to the environment by microplastics and plastics in the world's oceans, and we see that finding alternative means of closing the circle in plastics production is of the essence. Here are some projects that are underway (European Parliament, 2018–2023 and Enfield, 2018).

In 2012, the ambition of Carlos Monreal, CEO of Britain's Plastic Energy, was to improve plastic waste recycling. Together with scientists from Loughborough University, the company started looking into methods to process and convert all sorts of plastics into a fuel that can be used in cars and aeroplanes, or into hydrocarbons which can be used by chemical companies to make new plastics, thus closing the cycle. The research led to a so-called crack method (a process which involves heavy molecules being broken up into lighter ones) whereby heating up (rather than burning) the plastic delivers the 'original' fluid components.

At Chemelot, Plastic Energy and Sabic have built an installation which is the first in the world to produce certified circular polymers (Sabic, 2021). With these polymers Sabic (with DSM among others) can produce certified circular plastic packaging.

Meanwhile, DSM produces Dyneema, a strong fibre used in aircraft, cars, boats, fishing nets and in medical applications. This is traditionally made entirely from fossil raw materials but the company's goal is to make the fibre at least 60% sustainable in 2030. To achieve this, DSM and Sabic started a partnership with the Finnish timber company UPM Biofuels in 2020 (UPM, 2020). DSM also aims to collect and chemically reprocess products made from 'classic' Dyneema.

No success without setbacks

In 2019, licences and financing were arranged for the biggest bio fermenter in Europe to be built. The installation would convert 700,000 tonnes of pig manure, delivered by farmers in the Dutch provinces of Brabant and Limburg (3.5% of their total annual manure production), into biogas and phosphate, as a dry fertiliser. Fertiliser manufacturer OCI was to make its input more sustainable by using this biogas instead of natural gas: the residual heat would be delivered back to the fermenter. In this way, maximum energy efficiency with full recycling of all minerals could be achieved.

But there is no success without setbacks. In December 2020, the two companies announced that the project would not go ahead. None of those involved would explain the reasons behind this decision.

WHO WILL PICK UP THE TAB?

Making industry circular means letting go of the business and scientific ways of thinking which have made process technology increasingly more efficient. This efficiency has a price, and now that price has to be paid. The European Commission has identified hydrogen production as one of the most important pillars of green transition and has reserved hundreds of billions up to 2050 for it. But for answers to the questions of where, when and how much will be invested, we have to wait for plans and contributions from national governments and the business sector.

Table 11.1 Renewable energy, targets and results

Renewable energy in EU27 *(2021, as percentage of gross final energy consumption)*	
Top 5:	
Iceland	85.78
Norway	74.08
Sweden	62.57
Finland	43.09
Latvia	42.1
Bottom 5:	
Belgium	13.04
Netherlands	13
Malta	12.15
Luxembourg	11.73

Source: Eurostat.

NOTES

1 More of these bottom-up initiatives can be found on Sharingbrainpower.eu.
2 Brightsite Centre Geleen is an initiative of the University of Maastricht, TNO, Sitech Services and Brightlands Chemelot Campus (Chemelot, 2019).

REFERENCES

Chemelot (2019) Brightsite benoemt directeur en ontvangt opdracht voor eerste zes programmalijnen *(in Dutch)*. Available at https://www.chemelot.nl/nieuws/brightsite-benoemt-directeur-en-eerste-zes-programmalijnen (Accessed 5 September 2023).

Enfield, L. (2018) Does this Stratford tech company have the solution to single-use plastics? Available at https://www.inyourarea.co.uk/news/does-this-stratford-tech-company-have-the-solution-to-single-use-plastics/ (Accessed 5 September 2023).

European Parliament (2018–2023) Plastic waste and recycling in the EU: facts and figures. Available at https://www.europarl.europa.eu/news/en/headlines/society/20181212STO21610/plastic-waste-and-recycling-in-the-eu-facts-and-figures (Accessed 5 September 2023).

Renewable Carbon News (2021) Using plasma technology to feed the world *(quoting a TU Eindhoven press release)*. Available at https://renewable-carbon.eu/news/using-plasma-technology-to-feed-the-world/ (Accessed 5 September 2023).

Sabic (2021) SABIC and Plastic Energy set to start construction of pioneering advanced recycling unit to increase production of certified circular polymers. Available at https://www.sabic.com/en/news/26247-sabic-and-plastic-energy-set-to-start-construction-of-pioneering-advanced-recycling-unit (Accessed 5 September 2023).

Sederel, W. (2019) Sugar from sugar beets as building blocks for the chemical industry. Available at http://www.acrres.nl/wp-content/uploads/2019/07/W.-Sederel-Presentatie-Biethanol.pdf (Accessed 5 September 2023).

Sekab (2020) Sekab and Vertoro to build large-scale demonstration plant to produce a new platform for sustainable fuels, chemicals, and materials. Available at https://www.sekab.com/en/press-releases/sekab-and-vertoro-to-build-large-scale-demonstration-plant-to-produce-a-new-platform-for-sustainable-fuels-chemicals-and-materials/ (Accessed 5 September 2023).

TU Delft (2019) TU Delft, Shell and the government invest 5 million euros towards sustainable breakthrough in the chemical industry. Available at https://www.tudelft.nl/en/2019/tbm/tu-delft-shell-and-the-government-invest-5-million-euros-towards-sustainable-breakthrough-in-the-chemical-industry (Accessed 5 September 2023).

TU Delft (2020) TU Delft accelerating the electrification of the chemical industry. Available at https://www.tudelft.nl/en/stories/articles/tu-delft-accelerating-the-electrification-of-the-chemical-industry (Accessed 5 September 2023).

UPM (2020) DSM announces partnership with SABIC and UPM Biofuels to create bio-based Dyneema. Availabe at https://www.upm.com/about-us/for-media/releases/2020/03/dsm-announces-partnership-with-sabic-and-upm-biofuels-to-create-bio-based-dyneema/ (Accessed 5 September 2023).

Vaessen, W. (2016) Opportunities for the fermentation-based chemical industry: An analysis of the market potential and competitiveness of North-West Europe. Available at https://www2.deloitte.com/content/dam/Deloitte/de/Documents/Mittelstand/Deloitte%20Zukunftsforum%20Agrar%202016_Villem%20Vaessen__%20Fermentation%20Study%20Summary.pdf (Accessed 5 September 2023).

PART IV

THE DIGITAL TRANSITION

12

DIGITALISATION AND THE SEARCH FOR EUROPEAN STANDARDS

KEEPING DATA SHARING SAFE AND INDEPENDENT

We buy books via Amazon, we plan our routes and make appointments via Google, we share our daily lives with stories and photos on Facebook, we attend conferences and do job interviews via Zoom and we can call anywhere in the world for free via WhatsApp or Skype. Our cars have become computers on wheels. All this digital traffic creates a lot of data. Amazon was the first to exploit this with the Cloud, a global storage space for data.

Many politicians are by now aware that the digital transition has been taking place out of their sight, and that data has become a geopolitical tool. Europe, China and the USA are each taking measures to force major tech companies to make their data available to the secret services if national security is threatened – but also when the basic human right to privacy comes under fire.

In Brussels, privacy legislation to protect citizens has been introduced, but Germany and France want to go further. After negotiations with US tech companies to store acquired data in Europe were met with resistance, both governments have come to realise that the sovereignty of government organisations' and

DOI: 10.4324/9781032703381-17

companies' data should be guaranteed in systems that Europe itself must develop.

Europe is not going to build its own Google for this. But there is a need for a safe, reliable and intelligent space where data can be stored and shared. A 'local cloud' of sorts, where all contributors can keep their own software and remain owners of their data. The Answer: the IDS, Europe's own International Data Space.

Announcing a European cloud called GAIA-X (Grüll & Stolton, 2020–2022), in the summer of 2019, Peter Altmaier, then German minister of economic affairs, said that the dependence on Google, Amazon and others must come to an end. Europe should not be crushed between the Wild West and the Far East. A year later, a legal entity is formed for the project, in which 11 German and 11 French companies take part. At the moment, they are arguing over the question who is going to build the cloud software. The project consists of an association, hubs and an online community; all to encourage the digital sharing of know-how and innovation in a safe, non-centralised way.

Table 12.1 Digital Economy and Society Index

Digital Economy and Society Index, 2022	
Top 5:	
Finland	70
Denmark	69
Netherlands	68
Sweden	67
Ireland	63
Bottom 5:	
Slovakia	43
Poland	40
Greece	39
Bulgaria	38
Rumania	30

Source: Digital Economy and Society Index (DESI) 2022, from the European Commission.

Table 12.2 European digitalisation, facts and figures

European digitalisation, facts and figures		
In 2022:		**Target for 2030:**
54%	of Europeans aged 16–74 have at least basic digital skills	80%
8%	of EU businesses use AI	75%
14%	of EU businesses use Big Data	75%
70%	overall fixed high-capacity network availability	100%
56%	of the total 5G spectrum is assigned	100%
26%	of available recovery and resilience facilities is allocated by the member states to digital transformation	

Source: Digital Economy and Society Index (DESI) 2022, from the European Commission. https://digital-strategy.ec.europa.eu/en/news/digital-economy-and-society-index-2022-overall-progress-digital-skills-smes-and-5g-networks-lag

A SHORT HISTORY OF IDS

The impetus for building a neutral data space came from Germany. In 2013, a meeting between the government and major companies, software engineers, banks and smaller suppliers concerning the digitalisation of industry led to a strategic initiative called Industry 4.0. But it caused dissatisfaction among small- and medium-sized companies, who felt they had no choice but to follow the major players in this initiative.

Siemens then stepped in, claiming they had the software to build the desired digitalisation of industry. But to use this so-called 'Mindsphere' programme, which car manufacturers like BMW and Daimler already were using, meant that all existing software from suppliers other than Siemens had to be removed. These suppliers obviously reacted fiercely against this lock-in. A system developed by SAP was subject to the same limitations.

Time was pressing on; no further steps were taken. Then Google came to Munich, Siemens's backyard, with a polished presentation on what it could offer the industrial internet. The situation escalated into a national debate; representatives of the SMEs held their ground so that finally Prime Minister Merkel came to be involved. She took the plunge and decided that a secure digital space should be created in which data remains the property of the original owners. The task of coming up with an action plan was delegated to the Fraunhofer Institute.

In the autumn of 2015, Boris Otto, professor at the Technical University of Dortmund and head of Fraunhofer, publicly launched the *Industrial Data Space* project. The goal was to develop an architectural concept within two-and-a-half years that would allow the efficient exchange of data between those offering it and those using it. Reliability, digital security, data sovereignty and ease of use were pivotal. The concept's starting point was federal data management, meaning there was to be no central management or decision centre.

Connector software

In the set-up that Fraunhofer worked on in its second phase (since 2017), a *Connector* plays an important role. This is standardised software which is placed with the participating company or platform. It gives access to the digital space, makes the exchange of data possible and can make contact with other Connectors.

First tests centred around logistics and manufacturing. Volkswagen and Thyssen Krupp-Presta, its supplier of integrated car management systems, were amongst the first to try out the system as supplier and end-user. Early on, an alternative 'Smart Connected Supplier Network' (SCSN), built on Eindhoven's Brainport Industries Campus, proved itself to be a useful application for building a shared manufacturing data space, using the larger network of the IDS. The SCSN system is based on IDS standards; over 250 companies already use of it.

At that time, analysts had focused exclusively on the German situation. This is understandable but it was not long before the door was opened to other countries; when it comes to the digitalisation of industry, natural borders are irrelevant. The *Industrial* Data Space became the *International* Data Space. Since the beginning of 2016, companies, software developers and other organisations from Germany and Europe can become members of the newly established International Data Space Association (IDSA).

IDS SECOND PHASE: SHARING BRAINPOWER WORLDWIDE

In the second phase of the IDS project, Fraunhofer was tasked to establish connections with North America's Industrial Internet Consortium (IIC) and the Industrial Chain Initiative (IVI) in Japan. The IIC was set up in 2014 by, among others, IBM, Cisco and GE. Its aim is to provide a test setting to discover which protocols or standards can ensure safe data exchange. IIC sees as its most important task to develop the standards that US companies will adhere to when it comes to exchanging data. The Japanese initiative, started in 2015, was more loosely set up as a series of seminars to stimulate companies to explore new opportunities of digitalisation together.

The first joint research case (or *testbed*, as IIC calls it) was supplied in 2015 by Bosch and three other companies (Bosch, 2015). Bosch wanted to test the industrial use of a 'smart' screwdriver. Screws in an aeroplane, for example, must be accurately tightened or loosened depending on whether they are used in a wing or a window. A 'smart' screwdriver can provide an engineer with very specific information about its use. But who is owner of the data: the producer of the screwdriver or the builder of the airplane?

The five functions of IDS

Fraunhofer has created a number of functions. The 'Connector' is responsible for an ecosystem or chain of companies who wants to store their data. Next to this, there are the 'Broker,' the 'Clearing house,' the 'Identity supplier' and the 'App store.' The function of the Broker is to organise the delivery or purchasing of data. The Clearing house sorts out financial settlements. The Identity supplier regulates permissions to enter the digital room. And in the App store, apps are available to ensure optimal data flow processing. To further ensure security and privacy, it was decided to use blockchain technology within IDS.

FROM EUROPEAN STANDARD TO WORLD STANDARD

Industry 4.0 had another angle to it; one of its other aims was to set up a new industry standard for the digital era. As a result, the Standardisation Council Industry 4.0 is announced at the Hannover Messe in 2016. A reference system was presented along three axes. The first axis, which shows hierarchical levels, deals with how companies organise and control their IT systems. Internationally accepted standards for this already exist. The second axis – life cycle value stream – shows what phase a product is in. This goes from R&D to development, prototyping to production and sales to usage and maintenance. On the third axis are the functional layers that can be discerned in any product or machine (its business aspect, its function, integration, communication et cetera).

With this reference system, called RAMI, detailed discussions on any aspect of a technical process, product or machine can be aligned among European, Japanese, American and Chinese industry representatives. The reference system and SCI40 should result in the harmonisation of existing national models with the proposed three-axes model.

DATA SAFETY

The RAMI system provides every company with a level playing field in terms of data storage and data exchange. This is relatively simple when applied to closed production systems. The big challenge is that the digital transition has gradually created a finely woven system of almost infinite amounts of data, mainly coming from equipment and machines that are fitted with sensors (the so-called Internet of Things).

Modern-day industry production is characterised by the use of intelligent wireless sensors in anything from robots and machines, to vehicles and containers, to individual end products. This means that data communication is changing dramatically inside industry too. There is not always a clear overview of what is happening where; whether data is only used within a company or whether outsiders can also access it; which part of the data is in an external cloud and which is stored within the company's own data environment.

Can the current system of agreements and protocols be supplemented or adjusted so that global reference points emerge which can counter confusion, misuse, false competition and even cyber-attacks? And will the IDS be able to maintain its open character, whilst also supplying enough safety for its users? In the transitional phase that the manufacturing industry is currently in, negotiations at EC level have to be in step with the research that companies and knowledge institutions are carrying out in test locations. Questions of data safety, harmonisation, technical limitations and industry needs are all pieces of the puzzle which must eventually provide a complete picture.

BRAINPORT, NETHERLANDS: COMPLEXITY DRIVES COOPERATION

The circumstances for companies in the Dutch manufacturing industry are fundamentally different from those in France, Germany and Italy. In these countries, the car industry and mechanical engineering dominate. In the Netherlands, a specialist manufacturing industry has remained after many traditional heavy industries disappeared in the 1980s and 1990s. This specialist sector is characterised by low volumes, a high level of complexity, and cooperation by necessity.

The driving forces behind this high-tech manufacturing industry are five companies: Philips, ASML, FEI (Thermo Fisher), DAF and Océ (Canon). They are all located in the Eindhoven or nearby Venlo regions. Their products, such as medical diagnostic equipment, chip machines, electronic microscopes, copy machines and trucks, all require precision and flexibility.

When in the early 2000s, John Blankendaal, strategist for the Brabant province which incorporates Eindhoven and Venlo, heard local suppliers express their worries about the ever higher demands made on their products, he started talks with them. They came to the conclusion that the increasing complexity of new products and parts calls for cooperation or, in other words, Sharing Brainpower. During this period, the region of Eindhoven set up an innovative ecosystem with local councils in the surrounding area, under the ambitious name Brainport Eindhoven. Companies could join by pledging their cooperation to an association called Brainport Industries.

Blankendaal was asked to head the association. He believed that Sharing Brainpower should take place in a shared physical location. Brainport Industries premises were ready at the end of 2018. This is when I met him for the first time. As proud as a peacock, Blankendaal showed me around. In reply to my question of how he would avoid becoming a project developer only interested in renting out office space, he said with conviction: 'Only those who want to contribute to innovation, to the improvement of products and who are willing to share knowledge, are welcome.'

One of the successful Fieldlabs that emerged at Brainport Eindhoven, is the previously mentioned Smart Connected Supplier Network (SCSN – see box 'Connector software'). A normal data exchange between companies takes place via an EDI link; a standard electronic format that replaces paper-based documents such as purchase orders or invoices. But once in the cloud, a company's information is visible to the cloud service provider. However, many SMEs type in orders or other data into their own systems manually. This makes data difficult to share and, of course, increases the risk of mistakes.

In the new SCSN system, these disadvantages are solved. Companies just need to register once with an SCSN Service Provider. Then all data, such as orders, invoices, drawings and other technical product information, can be scanned, indexed, stored and exchanged with companies connected to the product chain. The company providing the data stays in control of it and decides to whom it is delivered.

DATA NETWORKS IN EUROPE: LESSONS ON SHARING KNOWLEDGE

IDS is operational since the summer of 2020. It is still mainly German companies such as Bosch, Siemens, BMW, Deutsche Telekom and Salzgitter that are making use of it; it is up to the IDSA to attract more European companies to make it a truly European data network. The German initiative to create a collective space for data exchange was nourished by its federal culture, which engages all those directly involved in the decision-making. By giving Fraunhofer the lead early on, both national and international politics have played virtually no role – the final plans were not mandated top-down.

With Brainport Eindhoven, too, the government kept itself at a distance. Brainport Industries' approach was more pragmatic than the German's worry about data becoming a geopolitical tool: 'If the cooperation we need to innovate can be supported digitally, let's just build such a structure and see how that holds up.'

It appears that this practical, bottom-up approach fits in seamlessly with the system thinking of Brainport's German colleagues. Both cases also show how existing institutes – Fraunhofer and TNO – have become the unique Connectors that can iron out any wrinkles and make new possibilities a reality.

CLOSING THE DIGITALISATION GAP: INNOVATION HUBS

European Commission research has found that there are big differences between countries when it comes to digitalisation. The Scandinavian countries are clearly at the front (Denmark is leading with companies which are over 50% digitalised) with the Netherlands close behind, but many countries in Central and Eastern Europe lag behind. At the moment, Greece is at the bottom with only 10% digitalisation in its companies. Across the board though, SMEs, even though they make up 99% of all business in the EU, are falling behind their larger counterparts.

Digital innovation hubs are part of the Digital Europe Programme, aiming to improve information security, strengthen Europe's position in the area of artificial intelligence and speed up the digitalisation of industry and society via hubs in the period 2021–2027. The budget is some 7.5 billion euros of which 700 million euros is reserved for the creation of the hub network.

Since 2018, the European Commission and member states have been setting up the network. Ministries of Economic Affairs in all the member states make a proposal to Brussels for what sort of hubs they would want to set up. Based on these proposals, the commission selects which hubs they will support. By bringing together companies, knowledge institutions, start-ups, accelerators, vocational colleges and technical universities in the region, new technical possibilities can be tested before businesses make an investment (European Commission, 2018). Another stated benefit is to have experienced staff and young students working together in the test facilities with the newest machines, so that experience is passed on.

These digital innovation hubs which the commission wants to introduce are a first step to the Fieldlabs in the Netherlands. In Eindhoven, John Blankendaal explained to colleagues from the Czech Republic, among other countries, how Brainport Industries involved its regional government, vocational colleges, universities of applied science and universities.

KEEPING CLOSE TABS

In 2022, the European Commission received 283 proposals from member states. In making the selection, attention is paid to the regional spread per country, the sectors that are represented (agriculture, industry, mobility, healthcare, services et cetera) and to the technologies that will be used: sensors, robots, 5G, blockchain, remote sensing and photonics.

At a minimum, every country will have to set up a hub or submit a proposal which fully focuses on artificial intelligence, a spearhead for the commission. These hubs receive financial support, but regional authorities – municipalities, provincial governments or regional development banks – and companies will have to take the lead.

The commission will follow the hubs, give advice and stimulate cooperation between hubs from different countries so all available knowledge is shared. In this way, cohesion between member states can be strengthened programme.

The EC also wants to select a restricted number of Testing and Experimentation Facilities (TEFs), focusing on manufacturing, healthcare, agro-food, communities and cities. With the introduction of the digital innovation hubs and the TEFs, a new institutional structure is growing in Europe, in which clever use is made of existing national knowledge institutions such as vocational colleges and universities. At the same time, regional authorities and SMEs are invited to join, so they can get a first-hand look at new digital technologies and share their experiences.

'How to make Europe greener and more digital are the twin challenges for our generation, and our success in meeting them will define our future,' according to the Digital Europe Programme. Digitalisation and data safety remain important goals within those challenges. But in 2020, the Corona pandemic created challenges at a more practical level of digitalisation: the global supply chains. China, the World's primary chips producer, issued its zero-Covid policy, causing severe delays and shortages. Brussels saw the need to reduce its dependence on China by opening its own chip production facilities.

A key question here is whether Europe should work to become an independent chip producer with the highest technological standards, or whether the EC should entice Asian and American companies to build factories here. The answer to that question is in the next chapter.

REFERENCES

Bosch (2015) Bosch is driving force behind first European testbed for the Industrial Internet Consortium. Available at https://blog.bosch-digital.com/wp-content/uploads/bosch-testbed-track-and-trace-industrial-internet-consortium-en.pdf (Accessed 5 September 2023).

European Commission (2018) Digital innovation hubs. Available at https://ec.europa.eu/futurium/en/system/files/ged/digital_innovation_hubs_in_digital_europe_programme_final2_december.pdf (Accessed 5 September 2023).

Grüll, P., Stolton, S. (2020–2022) Altmaier charts Gaia-X as the beginning of a 'European data ecosystem'. Available at https://www.euractiv.com/section/data-protection/news/altmaier-charts-gaia-x-as-the-beginning-of-a-european-data-ecosystem/ (Accessed 5 September 2023).

13

THE COMPUTER CHIP INDUSTRY

EUROPEAN ANSWERS TO INTERNATIONAL QUESTIONS

GROWING DEPENDENCIES

The Covid pandemic of 2020 exposed many global trading and production vulnerabilities. One of these was the research into, and production of computer chips. Europe's share of worldwide semiconductor production had already toppled from 25% to 8% since 2000 (Aurik, Gerdemann, Hales, 2022), so most of its chips already came from elsewhere – predominantly from China. But in 2020, demand was disrupted the US and European economies experienced a severe shortage. When economic recovery came unexpectedly fast and demand returned to old levels, it was the strict Corona measures in China that disrupted the supply. European car, refrigerator and washing machine manufacturers had to temporarily stop production.

To remedy these vulnerabilities, the European Commission took a first step at the end of 2020. This initiative, the European Initiative on processors and semiconductor technologies, would make up to 145 billion euros available to further the research, design and production capability of microprocessors in Europe. A little over a year later, the European Chips Act (European Commission, 2022) proposed a further 43 billion euros investment 'to prevent, prepare, anticipate and swiftly respond to any

DOI: 10.4324/9781032703381-18

future supply chains disruption.' The commission's measures should also bring Europe's share of worldwide production back to 20% in a growing market by 2030. The Chips Act was adopted in July 2023.

CAN WE DO THIS ON OUR OWN?

Thierry Breton, European Commissioner for the Internal Market, was eager to put Europe back in the 'driver's seat,' laying out a plan for Europe to catch up, both in production volume and in its nanotechnology. His key question to the sector was, Can we do this on our own?

No. This firm answer came from three key players, responsible for the smartest chip machines in the world. At the Hannover Messe in 2021, the CEOs of ASML, Zeiss and Trumpf distanced themselves from the ambition to build the entire chain here in Europe. According to them, the supply chain was incomplete and, moreover, Europe did not have enough funds to catch up with Asia.

This tech race was made all the more complicated because the other players weren't exactly resting on their laurels. Taiwan market leader TSMC was to invest 100 billion dollars in chip plants between 2021 and 2023. Washington allocated 52 billion dollars for its own Chip Act to support the American chip industry, with a leading role for Intel. Intel itself, the world's largest semiconductor manufacturer by revenue, was planning to build a new 20-billion-dollar factory in Columbus, Ohio, and vowed to catch up with Samsung and TSMC by focusing its research on the design and production of the smallest (3 nm) chips.

ASML TURNS THE TABLES ON THE EU

The day after the announcement of the European Chips Act in February 2022, a hitherto unthinkable public discussion on European industrial strategy started to unfold. ASML, the world's foremost chip machine maker, published a position paper (ASML, 2022) explaining why it would make sense to let either Intel,

Samsung or TSMC build an advanced production facility in Europe. ASML expected global chip demand to rise to 1,000 billion dollars within this decade. To expand the European share in this rapidly growing market to 20% 'requires significant public and private investments,' to the tune of 264 billion dollars.

ASML, while noting its satisfaction that the European Commission had set such an 'ambitious target,' stated that using Intel or Samsung as a 'springboard' would make much more sense, and would also serve to attract international talent. Start-up losses could be minimised with financial support from Brussels. The position paper then continued to inform the commission what steps to take. When Europe should take its advice not to develop the smartest chips on its own, the involvement of the commission should nevertheless remain strong. ASML therefore asked the EC to create a roadmap outlining the steps to be taken in the coming decades. Companies could tailor their investment programs accordingly.

In addition, ASML requested the EC to form an alliance, just as it did for the Battery and Hydrogen chains. This alliance should include established chip producers NXP (The Netherlands), Infineon and Bosch (Germany) and French-Italian STMElectronics. New chip producers would be welcome but, ASML added, only if they provided sufficient proof of a desire and ability to invest in an independent European production chain. The alliance should also include a growing group of end users: the biggest buyers of chips (Bosch, Continental, Ericsson, Nokia, Siemens, Philips and others). Research institutes like Fraunhofer, Imec and CEA-Leti would need to be included and would require financial support to further their research.

To remove all doubts and to reiterate its message to the EC, a concluding section of ASML's position paper neatly wraps up its main points:

- Europe needs a long-term 'semiconductor innovation roadmap' to guide investment decisions.
- To define this roadmap, a European Semiconductor Alliance should bring together manufacturers of semiconductors, their

customers in the major European markets, world-leading equipment and materials suppliers, research and technology organisations and policymakers.

- The roadmap should, in any event, support plans to:

    1. maximise the potential of European champions in semiconductor design, manufacturing equipment and materials, on which the global semiconductor ecosystem depends;
    2. invest in the European semiconductor ecosystem to boost Europe's strong industrial positions in global end-markets;
    3. invest in both mature and advanced semiconductor production in Europe;
    4. attract industry frontrunners to build advanced factories (or 'fabs') in Europe and
    5. upgrade European semiconductor process technology research facilities.

UPPING THE ANTE

Brussels did not explicitly gave reaction to this industry proposal – but the market did. Intel announced its own, ambitious, European investment plan in March of 2022. Investment should reach a total of 80 billion euros over the coming decade, giving the European digital ecosystem a much needed boost. A plant will be built in Magdeburg with 10 billion euros subsidy from the German federal government. The plan incorporated the building of new factories and labs in France and Italy and the doubling of capacity of existing production and research facilities in Ireland and Poland. In 2023, TMSC decided to invest in Dresden. NXP, Bosch and Infineon will each participate for 10% in this venture.

PHOTONIC CHIPS: EUROPE'S HIDDEN BEAUTY

Europe may be lagging behind in the production of traditional silicon chips, but it has a lead in the production of photonic chips, based on the use of light particles. Since data streams are continually increasing and computing is ever more energy-draining, it makes sense to research the data creation, transport and storage capabilities of photonic chips, which are faster, smaller and more energy-efficient than silicon chips. The telecom industry especially, holds great interest in photonic technology. Additionally, photonic chips can be used as sensors to detect vibrations in aircraft or infrastructures such as buildings and bridges, increasing safety and reducing maintenance cost.

The development of photonic chips is still in its infancy; production, quality control and packaging have not been well established. But research looks promising, and photonic chips are set to become a useful addition to silicon chips, and Europe happens to have a strong lead in the research into and production of photonic chips. The question at the moment is, Can technology standards and production methods be established quickly enough to maintain the lead? At the moment, 'prime movers' Belgium and the Netherlands are following two separate roads.

DIFFERING VISIONS

In the Netherlands, the technology that Ton Backx at TU Eindhoven and Richard Visser, formerly with Philips, have developed at Smart Photonics is based on indium phosphide. The company specialises on the production of photonic chips. Its technology allows the use of components such as optical amplifiers and light sources. EFFECT, another Eindhoven-based company using indium phosphide, claims it is the only company in the world that can build all elements of photonic chip technology. They focus on telecom and their technology can make use of existing fibre cabling. Chips currently sold cope with a relatively small amount of data (10 gigabyte per second) but EFFECT's clients are already thinking of one terabyte per second; for this, further research is necessary which its telecom partners actively contribute to (EFFECT Photonics, 2020).

But in Belgium, IMEC in Leuven and the University in Ghent stick to working with silicon. Their advantage is that there are already accepted world standards for silicon-based products. In

2006, professor Roel Baets of Ghent University set up xPIXfab, an initiative inviting the global photonics sector to pool knowledge and resources. Apart from speeding up research and reducing production costs of the chips, working together like this would be an easy way for the small researcher teams scattered around the globe, who rarely have adequate assembly facilities at their disposal, to access test and production resources (Baets, 2020).

So, how to create a leading world standard? The answer may be to combine the two routes described above. Based in Cork (Ireland), X-Celeprint has developed a technique that uses both silicon and indium phosphide. The EC already promised 5 million euros in subsidy to TU Eindhoven and IMEC, with the aim to have them find a joint platform that would perpetuate the technological lead that Europe has globally.

ADVANCING THE RESEARCH

Research and production of photonic chips can receive a further boost if the economic climate changes and the European production of chips becomes an even bigger focus point for the EC. Under the Chips Act, the commission has already increased the scope for granting state aid PhotonDelta for instance, an end-to-end value chain set up by Ton Backx that designs, develops and manufactures photonic chips, has already been granted 470 million euros by the EC, on top of the 600 million that PhotonDelta raised among companies and knowledge institutes.

Steps taken so far with the guarantee of continued funds from the government and companies are an important recognition for the companies involved. But the EU does not yet want to commit to any one technology.

KEEP THE FLAME BURNING

Daan Kersten, former CEO of PhotonFirst, welcomes the steady inflow of funds, but urges governments to act as launching customers, because, he says, 'a young company needs orders.' Maintenance of government buildings, roads and other infrastructure could become more predictable with sensors from his company; they could boost government efficiency. For his part, the feedback provided by the launching customers could lead to technical improvements and focus further research.

Technologically, there is indeed still a lot of work to be done. Practically inclined as they are, TU Eindhoven has also found it opportune to closely involve prospective customers. In 2018, for instance, Dutch telecom concern KPN entered into a long-term research alliance with the Technical University. According to Ton Backx, it meant 'the Technical University of Eindhoven becomes an extension of KPN in the field of research. In this way you can focus on the solution of problems that are important to society.'

Research institutes have had to make ends meet for a long time. It can take a while before their research and technologies acquire the focus and applicability necessary to receive either government funding or orders from launching customers. The same goes for many starting (tech) companies. In Eindhoven, for instance, it was only when the founders of PhotonFirst were able to use a university-grade microscope with the aid of a voucher from a government investment plan that they were able to steer the course of the company towards success. It was the birth period of companies that now, some 20 years later, form the core of the Dutch photonics ecosystem.

But sometimes the potential is seen early on. In Delft, professors and researchers from TNO had joined forces in QuTech, with which they conducted research into the Quantum Computer. Their work was brought to the attention of Dutch politicians who quickly elevated this innovation to national icon. The EC was not long in responding and gave the project its Flagship status. In the next chapter, I will describe how this bottom-up initiative was so quickly embraced by the European Commission.

REFERENCES

ASML (2022) Europen Chips Act – ASML position paper. Introduction and full paper available at https://www.asml.com/en/news/press-releases/2022/asml-position-paper-on-eu-chips-act (Accessed 5 September 2023).

Aurik, J., Gerdemann, D., Hales, M. et al. (2022) Europe's urgent need to invest in a leading-edge semiconductor ecosystem. Summary and full report available at https://www.kearney.com/industry/technology/article/-/insights/europes-urgent-need-to-invest-in-a-leading-edge-semiconductor-ecosystem (Accessed 5 September 2023).

Baets, R. (2020) Silicium-fotonica: een toegankelijke technologie voor telecom- en sensortoepassingen *(in Dutch)*. Available at https://www.imec.be/nl/artikelen/silicium-fotonica-een-toegankelijke-technologie-voor-telecom-en-sensortoepassingen (Accessed 5 September 2023).

EFFECT Photonics (2020) EFFECT Photonics' optical transceivers tune into the market. Available at https://effectphotonics.com/insights/effect-photonics-optical-transceivers-tune-into-the-market/ (Accessed 5 September 2023).

European Commission (2022) Digital sovereignty: Commission proposes Chips Act to confront semiconductor shortages and strengthen Europe's technological leadership. Available at https://ec.europa.eu/commission/presscorner/detail/en/IP_22_729 (Accesed 5 September 2023).

14

QUANTUM COMPUTING

AN EU-SPONSORED 'SANDBOX' ECOSYSTEM

TECHNOLOGY DRIVES THE ECOSYSTEM

The bottom up development of the photonic chip eventually, after some 20 years, received the support of Brussels through the Chips Act. The research into the quantum computer, which also took shape in the bosom of a University, received the support of the commission much more quickly and successfully.

In 2012, TU Delft drew headlines worldwide with its purported discovery of the Majorana particle. Even though they amended and critiqued their findings later on, interest was raised with Microsoft and Intel, among others: TU Delft was definitely on to something here (Microsoft discontinued its participation in 2022).

In 2014, TNO and the Technical University of Delft decided to join forces under the name QuTech. In this initiative, aiming to research and build full-quantum computing and communication systems, the university would be responsible for scientific research and TNO for its technical feasibility.

DOI: 10.4324/9781032703381-19

Majorana: hype and hypothesis

In 2012, Professor Leo Kouwenhoven's team saw the Majorana particle during an experiment in their laboratory in Delft. It was a stunning discovery. In 1937, the Italian physicist Ettore Majorana hypothesised that a particle which also contains its own antiparticle was missing from the Standard Model of particle physics. Since then, there was a global search to observe this particle.

In 2012, the researcher in Delft conducted a successful experiment in which the quasiparticle could be seen. This particle is very stable, making it a good candidate for building a quantum computer. In 2020, however, Kouwenhoven sought publicity with his suggestion that something might have gone wrong in his experiment. In February 2021, he retracted his article. However, after an Integrity investigation, Delft University came to the conclusion that Kouwenhoven's observation could not be discredited. (They reappointed Kouwenhoven in 2023, some 7 years after he left Delft to work for Microsoft.)

QuTech became the heart of an ecosystem. Also in 2014, their research into the quantum computer wins the Dutch government's prize for ground-breaking innovation. Professor Kouwenhoven and his colleagues are confident that this status will open doors for them in Brussels. And indeed, in the spring of 2016, the European Commission announced that research into quantum technology would be given Flagship status and that it would make 1 billion euros available for joint European research up to 2026.

The funding not only stimulated research in Delft, but also elsewhere in Europe. In Austria, a startup from the University of Innsbruck set to work on a quantum computer that could be used for chemical analysis and complex portfolio management. In Paris, a startup focused on a supercomputer to be used in a collaboration between the German Research Institute Julich near Aachen, and the French CEA, both eager to expand their computer power.

The ecosystem in Delft became more complex when in the autumn of 2016, Microsoft announced the opening of a fifth international laboratory called Station Q at Delft TU. Kouwenhoven would become its director. From that moment on, the crucial search for the stabilisation of qubits was taking place along multiple lines, through the Microsoft laboratory and QuTech.

Microsoft is the second American company active in the Delft ecosystem. Intel had already joined in 2015. It had invested 44 million euros in QuTech and supported work on 'silicon spin qubits.' Extremely cold (–273 degrees Celsius) electronics are needed to manage and measure these qubits, and Intel has experience in this field. In 2017, this co-creation led to the manufacture of a 17-qubit chip which was tested under extremely cold conditions.

Quantum computer basics

The Delft ecosystem is working on a computer that will perhaps take 20 years to be operational, but its accelerated processing power has the potential to lead to the discovery of new medicines and new materials. Current computers are based on bits, which are filled with a 1 or a 0. Quantum computers make use of qubits (quantum bits) which can be filled with a 1 *and* a 0, a doubling of value that is also called a *superposition.*

Qubits can influence each other even though they may be far apart: this is called *entanglement.* As a result of entanglement and superposition, multiple calculations can be done simultaneously. Processing power is doubled with every qubit that is added to the system. The technological challenge is to stabilise the qubits because temperature fluctuations, magnetic fields or the influence from nearby atoms may mean that the sustainability of the qubit is quite short. As a result, the currently available quantum computers are noisy: they are only useful for a limited set of computing problems (Hoving, 2018).

BRINGING IN BOTH USERS AND BUILDERS

'Quantum' is still very much in a technology-push phase; the search is dominated by scientists and technicians looking for solutions without being able to consult potential clients. How can you still broaden your vision? Aware of this necessity, QuTech brought in Kees Eijkel. He had worked for TU Twenthe for 35 years, commercialising technology, setting up a science park for technical start-ups. In Delft, he was appointed QuTech's business development director.

In 2020, QuTech launched Quantum Inspire. It is the first European quantum computer platform on which all those interested in doing so are invited to share their knowledge with each other by writing algorithms (Qutech, 2020a). At its official opening, Eijkel said: 'Experiencing a completely new technology first-hand will lead to a better understanding of the use value of these systems, and will increase society's acceptance.' But, he adds, 'Quantum Inspire will also work as a magnet to attract researchers, companies and start-ups. It can become a crystallisation point to a whole supply chain.'

Eijkel is the Connector between the university and the business community. Shortly after his appointment as business development director in 2018, a cooperation agreement was signed between QuTech and KPN, and three other parties. Telecoms provider KPN is one of the first logical future users of the quantum internet. But the company also provides useful research material: to test the connection between various quantum processors, which had already been achieved at laboratory level, a functioning quantum network has to be built. The high-speed glass fibre network KPN already laid out, can be used to this end. QuTech's researchers also hope to answer the question of how operators such as KPN think the quantum network can be used and with which services they want to approach their own clients (Qutech, 2020b).

Promising as the involvement of established parties like KPN may be, start-ups are an important instrument of commercialisation in the current early stage of this technology. This fact, Eijkel agrees, calls for improving the growth of healthy start-up propositions and a healthy investment climate. Since European corporations are lagging behind in investing in the technology, compared to the USA and some Asian countries, the start-up route is even more important.

THE DANES HAVE WIND, THE DUTCH HAVE QUANTUM

Not only the EU has awarded Quantum Computing flagship status. In the Netherlands, the ecosystem has grown substantially with the creation of Quantum Delta NL, at first a joint research project between five universities but at present 'a broad cooperation of knowledge institutes, companies and societal organisations. This ecosystem is organised in five hubs in Delft, Eindhoven, Leiden, Twente and Amsterdam, and covers all of the Netherlands.' In Amsterdam, Quantum Delta works closely with companies that select industrial use cases. In Leiden, the focus is on quantum chemistry. With financial support from Shell, Leiden tries to establish if complex molecules can be mapped with a quantum computer. In Twente, the focus is on nanotechnology, with which quantum applications and especially quantum photonics and quantum electronics are developed. In Eindhoven, the research focuses on new light frequencies, with help from startups and from Thermo Fischer (electronic microscopes).

The National Growth Fund, which the Dutch government has set up to enable future innovations, has honoured a widely supported request from Quantum Delta NL, allowing 632 million euros to be available until 2027.

REFERENCES

Hoving, D. (2018) The quantum computer exists, and it doesn't. Available at https://www.tudelft.nl/en/delft-outlook/articles/the-quantum-computer-exists-and-it-doesnt (Accessed 19 October 2023).

Qutech (2020a) Minister Ingrid van Engelshoven and European Commissioner Mariya Gabriel launch Quantum Inspire. Available at https://QuTech.nl/2020/04/20/minister-ingrid-van-engelshoven-and-european-commissioner-mariya-gabriel-launch-europes-first-quantum-computer-in-the-cloud-quantum-inspire/ (Accessed 5 September 2023).

Qutech (2020b) QuTech, KPN, SURF and OPNT join forces to build a quantum network. Available at https://QuTech.nl/2020/11/25/QuTech-kpn-surf-and-opnt-join-forces-to-build-a-quantum-network/ (Accessed 5 September 2023).

PART V

SHARING BRAINPOWER AS A WORKING MODEL

15

DRACHTEN CASE STORY

THE WEALTH OF DIFFERENT PERSPECTIVES

Building alliances is an art. There is no plan that you can implement; it is often a process of trial and error. But you can learn from the people and companies that have gone before you.

Building alliances is often a process from the bottom up, regionally or within companies. It is apolitical and very much driven by a desire to find solutions to practical problems. A new way of working together often evokes resistance at first; management feels sidelined or the Sharing Brainpower project is at odds with the company structure, in terms of hierarchy, information flow or remuneration. A marketer or buyer, for instance, is often rewarded if they buy as cheaply as possible, but in a new alliance, cost prices are regularly calculated in an integral way, so that in the long run the company will be better off.

When the European Commission talks about building alliances, it invites entrepreneurs, scientists, professors and local politicians to outline their plans. There usually is a lot of lobbying involved because there is much money to distribute. National politicians will show ambitious investment plans to indicate how seriously they take the proposed alliance. But in these EC alliances, eventually the parties will have to get down to business and find solutions to practical problems.

DOI: 10.4324/9781032703381-21

In this chapter, I focus on the Drachten case. In this provincial town in the north of the Netherlands, an alliance was built that cleverly (and fortuitously) avoids many of the pitfalls associated with Sharing Brainpower. For one thing, from the very beginning, as many disciplines as possible were involved in the process. People from finance, human resources, marketing, sales, software developers and engineers participate in determining and developing research projects, using their knowledge. In Drachten they call this 'anchoring the alliance deep within the company.'

FORCED TO BECOME SMART

In Drachten, a visitor will not find beanbags, foosball tables, hipster bars or other exponents of the current startup mentality. Drachten takes you 50 years back in time. Around lunchtime, men in blue overalls with a plastic sandwich box walk to the factory canteen.

But behind that traditional facade lies a new world of collaboration and knowledge sharing. Thoughts about external cooperation and anchoring activities in the region first came up within Philips management at the beginning of this century. They headed the local branch where, among others, electric razors were produced, and watched with regret as an entire production line was outsourced to China. They started to ask themselves how a further slimming down could be prevented.

At first, they started to compete on cost. Standardisation and automation were introduced; hundreds of low-skilled workers lost their jobs, which hit hard in the close-knit society. But in 2008, the Consumer Lifestyle research department was established in Drachten. As a result, around a third of its 2,000 employees are now engineers or product developers. In that same period, a sort of cultural revolution took place in the commercial department. Philips' traditional thinking in terms of technical superiority – 'we make the best products that we know to be good for the customer' – was abandoned; from that point on, the wishes of that customer came first.

ANY ALLIANCE STARTS WITH A CUP OF COFFEE

In building the Drachten alliance, two roles were important: first, that of the Connector, who has a vision of what the alliance should aim for, and knows how to inspire enthusiasm for a new working culture. Second, that of the Operator, who creates an efficient structure aligning with the goals of a project and is able to walk the talk.

In 2013, Philips management started to actively reach out to other companies. Then CEO Kor Visscher wanted to create an environment in which people would be continually stimulated to keep learning; and it was with this open, generous attitude that he proceeded. He opted for a low-key approach and started to invite colleagues from other companies out for a cup of coffee. His passionate story prompted similar personal revelations from his partners. He established a personal 'click' that reeled several companies in.

Visscher was the Connector who could paint a vision of the future, but he could also translate that to the here and now. He realised that the main danger in the process of building an alliance was Philips itself. He wanted to prevent his employer from becoming the big tree taking away the sunlight from smaller plants. From the start, he created a lot of space for the ideas of other participants. He regularly visited colleagues and asked what problems they were running into or what issues they wanted to investigate.

But Visscher wanted to do more than just bring companies together. He also wanted Drachten itself, the municipality of Smallingerland and the provincial government of Friesland to be involved – and they now are, wholeheartedly. To his mind, an indispensable link in the alliance is vocational education, from secondary school to polytechnic and university level. His motto is: Technology is not something you are taught about, it's a tool you have to work with.

PAY ATTENTION TO CULTURE

The cluster started with five companies in 2013 and grew to more than 20 in a couple of years. An association was set up with Visscher as Chairman (he retired in 2018). Legal expertise came from a lawyer who had once worked for Philips; she was asked not to make it too complicated. All the members of the association are part of the management team and everyone has just one vote, however large their company is.

Initially, Visscher devoted a lot of attention to creating an open culture, with room for each other's views and opinions. Give regional partners full credit, remain open-minded and continually be curious, share facilities, create a common structure for thinking about technical development and help others see that R&D does not have to be expensive: these are his most important lessons.

Other lessons are:

- Make sure that project proposals are coming in from all participants; prevent a leading party from becoming dominant.
- Make it clear that a project cannot be part of a company's core activities – but be aware of what their true needs are.
- Keep discussions practical and focus on results.
- Place responsibility as low as possible within the organisation and continually remind project leaders of this.
- And finally: draw up a non-disclosure agreement and a consortium agreement for each project.

The cluster grows steadily. At most one new company per annual quarter is allowed to join. Says partner Joost Krebbekx: 'There are always parties eager to join, but then they stand on the sidelines. Before you know it, you've got a management mentality, with meetings about procedures rather than active discussion about the projects.' For this reason, the association maintains a high standard of admittance. First, they judge whether a company fits within the agenda of the cluster and whether it adds new knowledge. Then follow talks with several people from the company. This strict policy has worked exceptionally well up to now.

COMBINING DIFFERENT POINTS OF VIEW TO WIDEN THE SCOPE

As a Connector, Visscher knew he needed assistance; he found Joost Krebbekx (mentioned above), a consultant from Dutch consulting agency Berenschot. After studying aviation engineering, he had worked for Philips in Drachten. He lives in nearby Heerenveen and has a comprehensive network among SMEs in the northern Netherlands. Acting as the programme manager of the cluster takes up about half of his time.

The research work flow is as follows: Every two years, a roadmap is drawn up by a steering group in which all participating companies have a seat. From the start, the technological areas of interest have been 3D metal printing, robotics, camera techniques, big data and neural networks and emission-free systems.

Krebbekx introduced a simple methodology. First, a longlist is put together by the steering group, which gets whittled down to a shortlist of five projects which will be worked on in the coming five years. There is special attention to whether all the parties in the decision-making process are on board and will remain so. The selected projects are managed as standard company projects, working from the generic idea to the specific elements and then back to the generic level. This creates a way of thinking which enables a network of people to understand each other. In the process, all participants, the smaller companies also, learn to manage complex projects.

Then, planning changes into doing. From this moment on, there are between 40 and 50 people involved in a typical project. The project has to grow roots deep in each organisation; it must not become a 'plaything' of those involved in the steering group. HRM, engineers, software, commercial/marketing and financial departments – all must be committed. In this way, a broad range of insights and ideas are expressed and reckoned with. Once every six weeks, the steering group comes together and evaluates the progress of around 40 projects. The meeting does not last longer than 1.5 hours.

Projects, of course, cost money. The hours worked are registered and are valued each at 60 euros. Of this payment, half comes from the Smallingerland municipal subsidy; the provincial government also subsidises the cluster. In this way, out-of-pocket costs and the hours any company puts into a project are kept under control. Krebbekx: 'Also, in this way people who are involved in the project are constantly thinking about how to keep the project alive. Taking the long view but paying out the hours spent keeps people invested and forward-looking.'

LEARN FROM YOUR LEGACY

Sharing Brainpower in Drachten is organised in such a way that all existing knowledge is used. In other words, people are taken seriously. Whichever discipline they represent, they are included in the whole process of development. If resistance is met, people will not complain or talk behind each other's back, but engage in discussion to find out what can be done differently and what may work better.

Due to the involvement of many disciplines, the scope is broad, but there is still a strong focus in Drachten. This focus on the technological issues at hand is cherished, because it prevents the alliance from becoming a group of industrial dreamers or, at the other end of the spectrum, becoming bogged down in discussions about managerial matters.

The involvement of local authorities and vocational training schools does wonder to keep companies rooted in the region, and it offers the schools the opportunity to put taught skills to practical use. The University of Groningen recently decided to establish a master's programme in Mechanical Engineering on the Philips premises. This was a unique decision, because universities are often picky in their connections with the world of business. They will attract companies to carry out part of their research; or they seek out businesses to put their research into practice.

In the next chapter, I'll discuss more general ways in which Sharing Brainpower can take shape. But whichever form it takes, trust and generosity are central.

A MENTALITY OF CO-CREATION

In Drachten, a few companies started looking into the possibilities of new technology. The local government supported the initiative, and vocational schools and other knowledge institutions sent young, eager students. The mix of insights and perspectives was increased by allowing the research findings to sink deep into the companies. In less than ten years, an ecosystem has emerged there that is essentially a research network into the Factory of the Future.

Drachten is a comprehensive example of Sharing Brainpower. Early on, founder Kor Visscher had a strong, enduring vision of what the Drachten alliance should achieve. Operator Jeroen Krebbekx proves able to guide all existing and new partners towards these shared goals. But there are also examples in which a simpler approach is chosen, which also show the power of Sharing Brainpower.

- At vehicle technology company ZF in Germany, the use of Data Science was operationalised in cooperation with the nearby University of Freiburg.
- At BMW, promising start-ups are brought into the company and are given a sales market within the automotive business.
- ABP, the largest pension manager in the Netherlands, wanted to make its systems more flexible with a view to social

DOI: 10.4324/9781032703381-22

individualisation. The company had no experience in R&D, so in a short time, it built an ecosystem with external knowledge parties.

- Four business friends, sharing their frustration over millions of spare parts produced redundantly in each of their companies, decided to join forces to digitise the inventory management of spare parts. With 3D printing, any part can now be ordered globally from their company.
- In Eindhoven, two entrepreneurs without any technical knowledge started a company to build a 3D metal printer, using available knowledge in the regional ecosystem.

All of these, purposefully random, examples show that Sharing Brainpower requires a mentality of co-creation, of realising your own expertise falls short of your goals. But learning to think integrally from different perspectives that often contradict each other is a major challenge. In this chapter, I will highlight some issues and questions associated with (starting) the process of Sharing Brainpower. The five examples will be explored below.

ASKING QUESTIONS BECOMES THE NEW CULTURE

Sharing Brainpower requires a new culture in which asking questions becomes the most normal thing in the world. That may sound obvious but it isn't. At *Het Financieele Dagblad,* I made it common practice that interns would attend both the editorial morning meeting and the afternoon front-page meeting. During job interviews, I asked them to take active part in any discussions. A colleague of mine, who grew up in the USA, told me once that this would be impossible at an American newspaper. I answered that I found the fresh views of young, upcoming journalists beneficial because they still thought outside of our own established patterns.

Hierarchy is still entrenched in many company cultures. This became all the more clear to me when I talked to a friend about the cooperation between Air France and KLM. He was regularly in France to talk about the integration of their activities. What he noticed was that French managers were never contradicted during a meeting. If there were issues, they would be approached after the meeting by a colleague responsible for a particular file; after this talk, corrections could be made. A senior executive views contradiction as criticism and that is 'not done' in French boardrooms.

Relationships in a cluster or alliance are different. They are less formal because they are about work being done within the framework of a project. That requires a solutions-oriented attitude. In this way, alliances can be the breeding ground for the cultural adjustments needed to make rigidly organised, hierarchical companies more flexible and open to change.

LEARNING FROM DIFFERENT PERSPECTIVES

In February 2017, I met professor Alan Broadfoot, a Connector if ever there was one, in Newcastle on the West coast of Australia.[1] He was in charge of the energy research institute NIER at the University of Newcastle. Six years previous, the biggest raw materials company in the world, BHP, had decided to sell off its research department to the local technical university. BHP left a part of its research behind.

I asked Broadfoot how the cooperation between an independent institute and a commercial company was going. The tension implicit in this cooperation was something I felt intensely, because at the media concern where I had worked my whole life (journalistic) independence was considered sacrosanct. However, without advertisers and subscribers, your existence was at risk.

Broadfoot: 'You can talk endlessly about how much independence you have given up. But what I have learned is that a research question from a private company – not only BHP but others too – offers an unexpected perspective. Our existing know-how is used in a different way and we arrive at new insights.' Broadfoot has both a warm heart for science and a practical spirit; he views working with a commercial party simply as a way to gain new insights.

In Drachten, Connectors have consciously chosen to bring together a whole chain of perspectives. Kor Visscher talked about his passion for bringing together people and companies who do not just talk about new technology but actually work with it. In his story of how a cluster is created, he never used the word diversity. But this is exactly what was at the heart of the Drachten case: functional diversity.

This was achieved by embedding partnerships deep in the organisation. Marketing, commercial activities, financing, maintenance, human resources and technicians were all involved in the projects. Also, a wide range of educational institutions were members of the cluster. It is this layering of perspectives that makes for an extremely interesting learning process, for example, in the search for ways to advance the digitalisation of production processes.

INVITE START-UPS TO SET UP WITHIN YOUR COMPANY

How does a large, well-established company keep an eye on newcomers that introduce disruptive technologies onto the market? Over the last decades, a growing number of companies have set up funds to invest in promising start-ups. Companies like Denmark's Maersk, Germany's Siemens, France's Schneider Electric and Finland's Wärtsilä have all set up such a business venture company.

BMW has also set up an investment fund, but the company went even further. Their starting point is simple, but far-reaching in its consequences. Instead of only investing in promising start-ups, outside entrepreneurs are invited to team up with BMW clients and are paid for future deliveries of their new products. This so-called Startup Garage was introduced by Gregor Gimmy, a serial entrepreneur in Silicon Valley and Matthias Meyer, who worked for years as an engineer for the German car maker (Gimmy et al., 2017). Naturally, this process requires a lot more trust in the capabilities and the loyalty of new, outsider entrepreneurs – but the rewards for BMW and its clients will be all the greater too.

For a project like the Startup Garage to succeed, top management must embrace the idea – but innovation management and other relevant departments must also stand behind it. Through a dedicated website, guest lectures at relevant universities and warm contacts with private venture funds, the search for the right start-ups began. To be eligible, the start-ups had to have a trusted team and a working prototype of their product. The preparatory work – selection, financing and writing of a business plan – is done by the private venture funds. When a suitable party is found, a pilot project is initiated.

In the Startup Garage, entrepreneurs do not have to hand over shares to BMW: there are no strings attached! They are introduced to the relevant departments into which their product will be integrated. In these pilot projects, young enthusiastic minds meet the experienced forces that can best predict the impact of new products on the rest of the process.

Once the proposal for a test project is accepted by the implementing department, Startup Garage issues the start-up with a supplier number and a purchase order, which means its trustworthiness within the BMW logistics is guaranteed.

Startup Garage's freedom to act outside of official purchasing channels – which relieves the requirement of lengthy tendering processes – has resulted in a big boost to the whole innovation process. In the summer of 2017, 90% of the start-ups that had been part of the Garage scheme, met the expectations of the BMW directors.

CHERISH THE LEGACY OR START AFRESH?

In the context of the three transitions that structure this book, how can you approach a switch to alternative energy sources, CO_2 reduction and waste elimination? What does digitalisation mean in the specific case of one company or organisation? And if you are committing to change, do you view your history as a source of inspiration for renewal or do you distance yourself from that past?

These, admittedly big and abstract, questions come into play one way or another when setting up an alliance. It's about changing your focus to single product lines within, or even new to, your company. It's about letting go of established hierarchies.

It can actually be a matter of reinventing yourself, similar to the well-known example of Nokia.

Danish energy company Orsted was very determined and distanced itself as much as possible from fossil fuels and concentrated on wind energy. Philips took leave of its lighting division – the foundation of its entire legacy – and moved on with medical appliances. Siemens put the majority of its resources into software developments for industry and wind energy. Lighting, chip technology and medical apparatus were publically listed.

The decision to let go is rarely an easy one. Unilever, a major user of palm oil, is committed to make its whole chain more sustainable. Dutch journalist Jeroen Smit documented Unilever's struggle to rebuild its legacy in his book *Het Grote Gevecht* (The Big Fight). He describes how former CEO Paul Polman negotiated with government leaders in Southeast Asia to leave the tropical forests undisturbed and not use them to create profitable palm plantations; how labour conditions of the palm oil farmers had to be improved and how the company's own employees had to absorb sustainability into their daily routines; how Polman ended up at the UN, where he made a plea to make the palm oil chain sustainable. The process is not yet complete.

In 2021, Shell lost its trusty shareholder ABP, the Dutch civil servants' pension fund, because Shell's transition was deemed too slow. The activist shareholder Third Point called on Shell to split up the company. However, Shell is convinced that its fossil activities are still necessary to pay for the transition to sustainability. In the last few years, the company has invested wholeheartedly in wind, solar and hydrogen.

But it's not just innovation and processes changing slowly at Shell. There are cultural and branding issues as well. Traditionally, Shell always prided itself in how its engineers had created and implemented complicated technological innovations, such as LNG and Gas to Liquids, in just 20–30 years. The Shell brand symbolised combined technological efforts to keep the unpredictability of nature under control.

Concurrent with this, Shell is slowly adapting to creating a more advisory role for itself. From its headquarters in London, a global network is being built of companies that want to reduce their CO_2 emissions. How do you make a car fleet greener, how do you reduce your data centre's energy consumption? Shell aims to add its know-how and experience to accelerate transition in this way.

When it comes to sustainability, Shell has to learn to look from the outside in. Here, too, are lessons to be learned from how Philips in Drachten had made the same switch. Like government, citizens, other companies and universities, Shell must learn how to reduce emissions.

These are just some examples. Many companies are not in a hurry to let go of their legacy. For a long time, companies thought that if the government provides the right framework, solutions will automatically present themselves. The answers would be technological and the government would have to force buyers and clients to accept the solutions. But the complexity of the three transitions is not only solved by a government that maps out clear social goals. Under pressure from the environmental NGOs and public protests, companies are forced to look at the effects of their business model on clients, buyers and the environment. For many, this is a new phenomenon.

HOW TO DEAL WITH INTERNAL RESISTANCE

In the mid-1990s, the publishing world was shaken up by new commercial media such as CNN and Sweden's free *Metro* newspaper. The internet was still in its infancy but it was not long before it became clear that this new medium made the accessibility of information cheaper and, in many cases, free. At the time, *Het Financieele Dagblad* was a newspaper aimed at (financial) functionaries and civil servants. Being first with the news was not a priority, 'FD' prided itself in in-depth information. Reader surveys indicated that more than 90% of our readers were men. Investors, business people and accountants passed along a single company copy of the paper at work. At the top right-hand corner of the front page, a note was stapled with the names of the next readers. Still, company subscriptions were the lion's share of sales.

When I became editor-in-chief in 1995, I wanted to make a newspaper for men and women who wanted to know how money was spent and how that influenced the world. The paper should be delivered to homes. The latest news should be combined with in-depth coverage. The financial focus should be preserved, but the scope of topics should be widened. With this vision, I opened the editorial discussion.

I was expecting resistance from the commercial department: FD had a unique position in the advertising market because we reached a small but coveted group of decision-makers. What surprised me was that the editorial department joined forces against my plans. Wouldn't they be the ones who would understand me best and support my analysis? I felt an angry frustration rising inside, but I knew that going head-to-head would not bring us any further.

So I asked myself what had gone wrong in the process. Why did they have the feeling that I was trying to take 'their newspaper' away from them? That I was trying to make a general-interest newspaper? In individual talks with colleagues, I came to realise that I had simply presented a solution, rather than an analysis of why I thought the changes were needed. Better still, I should have asked my colleagues to look at their own situations and use them to inform their views.

How do working parents deal with childcare? Is part-time work a blessing or a curse? How is the internet influencing the news supply? What does the social pressure to be more sustainable mean to your work? Gradually, it became clear that we had to put ourselves in the shoes of our target audience, the entrepreneurs or investors, when we interviewed them. Very gradually, editors and journalists learned that there is a whole world behind financial statements, a world that they themselves are also part of. The scope and tone of interviews changed because everyone was able to add something from his or her own experience.

The lesson I myself learned was that resistance can be the first step of a creative process. Don't start with solutions, rather make a connection to everyone's personal experience. When I translated the abstract concept of my proposal to their personal experiences, the idea started to come to life. Now, some 30 years later, *Het Financieele Dagblad* covers all aspects of the economy, business and society. Its focus is equally on the effects and personal stories around business and financial matters, and on the reporting of facts and figures. FD is read in the office and at home, and is also available digitally.

THE HORIZONTAL ENTERPRISE

To fully co-operate in a project, companies – especially established companies – must make an internal transition in order to release potential know-how and strength. This means flexibility in thinking and therefore flexibility in organisation. With an attitude of 'look beside you but keep your focus,' the horizontal enterprise is created, which uses this approach to expand its scope.

In a horizontal enterprise, people learn to look at things from different perspectives. This is possible on the basis of three 'co' concepts: co-creation, co-experience and co-learning. It is about learning to adopt a new mentality and attitude. In many organisations departments talk *about* each other, often in an accusatory tone. The trick is to get people from different departments to talk *to* each other and invite them to ***co-create***.

Belgian startup Showpad has designed a smart cloud system for this that brings together the know-how and expertise of the marketing department and salesforce. The system invites marketeers and salespeople to see each other as colleagues with the shared goal of serving clients. These sorts of tools are useful but it's important to realise that genuine cooperation is more than exchanging information.

A culture of cooperation can also be strengthened by allowing people to experience what the other has to offer – **co-experience**. At APG (see below), management coupled experienced operators with enthusiastic startup employees so they could learn from each other.

In the Netherlands, vocational colleges are increasingly taking part in innovation clusters. The country has over 40 Fieldlabs in which young people and experienced technicians work together with the latest state-of-the-art equipment. It is not unusual for a 15-year-old showing an experienced employee how to install a new lathe: an example of ***co-learning***.

SHARING BRAINPOWER WITHOUT R&D EXPERIENCE

What should you do if you have never done research and development as a company and still want to innovate? This was the case with Dutch pension fund APG. Its board of directors was intent on making its pension administration, which involves over 4 million clients, more flexible. So their question was, With which partners do we build that new system? The board asked Joep Beukers to take on the role of Innovator. After studying chemical engineering, he became a pension manager at APG through jobs at Philips and ING.

The first thing Beukers did was to work at building a co-creation mentality within the company. He did this, among other things, by training his sales and helpdesk personnel to view the traditional customer-supplier relationship in terms of a cooperation.

Second, Beukers established contacts with universities and startups. At that stage, he learns to deal with intellectual property and is struck by the enthusiasm of young entrepreneurs who have discovered a new algorithm or have written new software. Theirs are often innovations that work with small data sets. To make these techniques operational for the 4.5 million participants of the pension fund, he couples an experienced System Administrator with the young startup.

Finally, Beukers deliberately sought publicity. 'Let us know what you are working on, or what your ambition is. For example, by issuing a press release stating that you want to explore the possibilities of the blockchain.' It leads to a flurry of reactions from enthusiastic startups, from as far away as Australia and Canada. More parties are found and the combination of cooperation projects gradually leads to the desired flexibilisation of the system (The above sections are based on my article in Dutch: Bakker, 2018).

USING DATA SCIENCE IN A COOPERATION

In Ludwigshafen in the South of Germany, Niklas Goby is doing an internship at ZF, a supplier to the automotive industry. He studies Data Science in Freiburg, lands a position at ZF after graduation and after a few years, they also give him the time to do his PhD at his old university. With his PhD supervisor, he discusses how data analysis can be made useful for the company.

In a large company like ZF (146,000 employees), all eyes are focused on a new initiative: what will it mean for us, will it make us redundant? The first project has to prove itself to be an addition to the company's expertise, not a simple way to slash overhead. But at which department can ZF start, is it finance, logistics, sales, marketing or production? Where is the low-hanging fruit? Since there does not appear to be any, Goby and his supervisor make a case to look at the problems with the most impact and land at the production department.

Unexpected malfunctions in the product line result in work stoppages and cause inevitable problems for the operators. Despite limitations in the data, an algorithm is developed that prevents three-quarters of the malfunctions. This gives those on the product line a sense of security, they feel supported, not threatened by the new data-driven approach, and it saves the company hundreds of thousands of euros.

A next step to success is a cooperation with data scientists at the University of Freiburg. The support and expertise of this non-commercial external party in the pilot project led ZF to the realisation that innovation was no longer achievable through internal resources only. 'The future success of the company is partly dependent on what we can learn from working with an external party, but also from sharing knowledge and experience together,' says Andreas Romer, vice president IT Innovation at ZF.

The third step is crucial. Success would not have been possible if ZF's domain experts had not joined the cooperation. They had to provide the right insights on which good data depends. In many companies, this is often the bottleneck, because domain experts will feel they have been sidelined by external advisors or by the company directors; they are then unwilling to cooperate.

USING SHARING BRAINPOWER TO DEVELOP A NEW PRODUCT

Many entrepreneurs are aware of a lack of knowledge, or even data, to further their business. Some of them know that they are surrounded by an ecosystem based on sharing of knowledge. Eindhoven, the Dutch southern 'city of light' forever linked to the history of Philips, is such an ecosystem. With its Philips suppliers ASML (microchips), DAF (vehicles) and Canon (cameras, printers and other office hardware), the Eindhoven region appears to be an ideal place to develop a 3D metal printer.

The founders of what were to be called Additive Industries, Daan Kersten and Jonas Timmermans, were aware of their lack of technological prowess. A mini-congress that research institute TNO organised, with the cream of the crop of the region present, proved to be the ideal stage to announce their ambition. A little later, they invited a number of companies to do preliminary studies on the technical requirements that a metal 3D printer had to meet. These companies had no experience with 3D printing either, but were active in mechatronic subassemblies (hardware/software combinations that build machines for aircraft construction, healthcare, semiconductors and the food industry). They might become first customers. Kersten and Timmermans presented the association under the name AddLab.

But it took them a lot of persuading before the companies were willing to share their knowledge and free up manpower. The association only really got up and running when Mark Vaes, program manager Additive Manufacturing and system architect at TNO, started pulling the cart after six months. He suggested to visit potential buyers of the 3D printing machine, so they could tell him what a new machine from Additive Industries should be able to do better than, or beyond, what the competition provided. With this customer input, the company formulated its ambition, and within a year a prototype machine could be sent to the first client.

SHARING BRAINPOWER AS A START-UP ENTERPRISE

3D printers can save many other manufacturers from maintaining expensive stocks of spare parts. Spare parts involve a complex world of hundreds of thousands of items, imperfect administration and a general race to the bottom to have them as cheaply as possible made in China. Be it a washing machine, a car, an agricultural machine or an airplane, spare parts must be available for a long time, long after newer models have been introduced.

Tibor Melsem Kocsis, a long-time employee of Angst & Pfister, a Swiss company producing a wide range of machine parts to industrial partners, came upon the idea to digitise the inventory management and production of spare parts. Says Kocsis: 'Just think of these millions of items; you must keep them in stock but not everyone is used because demand is unpredictable. Over time, thousands upon thousands are simply destroyed, costing a lot of money and harming the environment.'

When Melsem Kocsis presented his solution to Amazon in Seattle, their reaction was enthusiastic. He was asked to cooperate with them. But back in the Netherlands, he told a few friends. Together, they decided to set up their own company (Jessayan, 2017). They already had the commercial and logistical know-how; what they lacked is a technical brain, a CTO. Eventually he was found: Alessio Nobile, an Italian living in Amsterdam. He was working at Customer Gauge, a company providing customer loyalty measurement software.

Once Nobile is on board, the company could be founded: they called it DiManEx, an abbreviation of Digital Manufacturing Exchange. Nobile started by designing a platform that provides insight into the entire process, from data analysis to the final delivery of the printed parts. Customer administration analysis provided the answers to questions like: Which parts, how are they made, from what material, are they trademark-free, how often are they requested, et cetera. Kocsis' partners started looking in Europe and the USA for 3D printing facilities that could produce spare parts in small quantities. Finally, some potential customers were visited and invited on the platform. In 2023, DiManEx had around 15 clients, including NS (the Dutch rail operator), the Dutch Defence ministry, Schneider Electric (France) and Electrolux (Sweden).

DiManEx's biggest challenge proved to be finding the right person to talk to. Sometimes they met buyers who would choose the 'path of least resistance': buying the cheapest items in China to receive a bonus for cutting costs. But Kocsis and his colleagues remain convinced 'cheap' is a relative concept; many buyers do not have to take storage costs into account.

DISCIPLINE, COMMITMENT – AND FREEDOM

The Drachten case teaches us that working together requires commitment. It begins when choosing new partners. They must be able to add intrinsic value to the selected research areas, so that meetings can continue to be about *projects* and not about *procedures*. A prospective partner needs to have proven experience in research. Do they have their own budget, their own director and a separate research department? This is a way to separate the wheat from the chaff, so to speak. Also, in Drachten there is a strict eye on cost inflation. Third, the legal foundations of any alliance should be sorted out in advance and be kept simple.

ZF, electronics supplier to the car industry, displays another way to ensure commitment and to create discipline: Ending a project must not be something that can be done easily. The internal data lab has found an ingenious solution: if a team wants to end a project, it must come up with the conditions under which it can be re-started. This way, more projects make it to the finish line.

Participants of Sharing Brainpower can also be kept focused by introducing a time limit on research projects. Projects financed by Brussels under the framework of Horizon 2020 are limited in scope and tied to a three- or four-year period. The same applies to the Fieldlabs in the Netherlands that are approved by the Ministry of Economic Affairs.

Being part of an alliance can feel like being in a gilded cage. It can be comfortable, with an exciting view and food for thought, but what to do if the cage starts to feel too small? Each participant has their own key to exit the cage. There has to be structure and discipline, but also freedom and a sense of responsibility. How do you make sure all remain committed? And when will the key be used?

Siemens and Evonik are very much aware of these issues. Both had invested years in developing their individual technologies. With Siemens' electrolyser, CO_2 can be transformed into hydrogen; Evonik developed a bioreactor in which a bacterial fermentation process transforms hydrogen into chemical input. The gilded cage both entered was a pilot project in which the electrolyser and the bioreactor were to be integrated.

This may lead to further steps along the way: after the chemical substance resulting from the integration is purified, further commercial uses are feasible. Do Siemens and Evonik continue together on this path, or will they go their separate ways again? Only through open communication at every step of the way, the needs, wants and responsibilities on both sides remain clear. The recent opening of Marl Chemical Park (Germany) is proof that up until now, the association has been mutually beneficial.

In Drachten, the selection of new participants is designed to rule out disappointment as much as possible. The criteria for new members are clear and talks are held not only with management but with all layers of the organisation. This appears to work. As of yet, none of the companies have used their key to escape from the cage.

WANTED: CONNECTORS

As stated earlier, Sharing Brainpower sometimes initiates a search for new forms of doing business. Connectors play a crucial role in that search. At an early stage, Kor Visscher felt a business and moral obligation to create a feasible local alternative which would make relocation to low-wage countries unnecessary. Through the cooperation he sought with other local producers, he built a cluster that became more firmly embedded in the region. It became a success, both in economic and in social respect, and most emphatically so when the University of Groningen opened a master's study on the Drachten site.

What many regions need are people who can see business opportunities or feel a moral obligation to take action and find a practical way to solve local challenges. I call these people Connectors; people who use their vision, passion, perseverance and creativity to take others, who are sometimes doubtful or hesitant, with them.

The Connector is a new sort of role model. When, at the end of the last century, Eindhoven was hit by the departure of traditional craftwork and the economic climate had dropped to zero, a small group of people stood up and called for the region to be turned into a high-tech centre. They were the dreamers. Some 15 years later, Eindhoven won a prize for being the 'smartest municipality' in the world.

Sharing Brainpower in ecosystems is increasingly seen as an effective way to solve technological, societal and ecological issues. The fact that you need Connectors (and Operators) to make it work, is also gradually acknowledged. The Connectors I have met have convinced me of the effectiveness and durability of Sharing Brainpower. Their mindset may be summed up as, 'We are looking at the same problem but we all see something different. By bringing our views and strengths together, we connect, we share, we build.'

NOTE

1 Caroline McMillen invited us gracefully for a two-week stay in February 2017. She was Vice-Chancellor and President of the University of Newcastle when she heard Antoine speak on BBC World News about the research collaboration between universities, startups and companies, a topic that was dear to her. We were keynote speakers at the annual meeting of the Australian Universities in Canberra. Professor McMillen retired in October 2018 and commenced the role of Chief Scientist for South Australia.

REFERENCES

Bakker, F. (2018) Overal wordt gebouwd aan allianties *(in Dutch)*. Available (through login) at https://fd.nl/morgen/1261264/overal-wordt-gebouwd-aan-allianties (Accessed 5 September 2023).

Gimmy, G., Kanbach, D., Stubner, S., Konig, A., Enders, A. (2017) What BMW's corporate VC offers that regular investors can't. Available at https://hbr.org/2017/07/what-bmws-corporate-vc-offers-that-regular-investors-cant (Accessed 5 September 2023).

Jessayan, H. (2017) Voorraad? Dat is iets van vroeger *(in Dutch)*. Available (through login) at https://fd.nl/morgen/1226677/voorraad-dat-is-iets-van-vroeger (Accessed 5 September 2023).

17

A NEW EUROPEAN APPROACH

Europe has decided to build on the strengths of its member states. This decision triggers a process which involves a search for qualities and knowledge that fit together. The three transitions in which we are currently involved require complex technological and social solutions that no one country can solve by itself. Those who want to partake in a solution need to have rich experience and knowledge, and a generous attitude. Instead of a project director dishing out tasks and orders, there is a need for a Connector who can bring together people with the right experience.

By choosing this approach, Brussels is initiating a new, less hierarchical, 'horizontal' way of working. This breaks with a long tradition, that started over a century ago in the Industrial Revolution, of organising human interactions around machines (processes) instead of around finished products (results).

With further development of technology, the steel industry, agriculture, chemicals, pharmaceuticals, aviation manufacture, the car industry and many more branches closed themselves off in their own worlds; few ever looked over the fence. When companies grew in size and scope, this process of creating 'silos' was also put to practice within businesses. First in the USA and later elsewhere, universities and business schools focused on ways to improve existing practices. Those were the glory days of so-called 'spreadsheet management.'

DOI: 10.4324/9781032703381-23

SEARCHING FOR COLLECTIVE GOALS

Sharing Brainpower signals the introduction of a new instrument to galvanise the supply side of the economy. A first result is that companies have joined forces – often including knowledge institutions and local government in the mix. The European Commission rewards this trend because it aligns with the EC's goals of making digitalisation safer and more autonomous, reducing CO_2 emissions and moving away from our dependence on fossil energy. By formulating these societal goals, Brussels is supporting Sharing Brainpower and creates the contours of new markets – which have already established themselves in the cases of batteries and hydrogen.

Building the alliances that are to become the foundation of the European Commission's policy, calls for all parties involved to understand what they are good at, but also where they fall short. Where do you complement each other, and how do you make the collaboration profitable, are questions that follow.

This may sound logical enough, but it requires a radical new way of looking at one's surroundings. It requires companies to look beyond the perimeter of their own defined work terrain, their compartmentalised sector, to focus on the world beyond. A century of compartmentalised thinking has saddled us with a handicap.

With the European Commission's decision to achieve the three transitions via alliances, they are inviting companies, universities and local governments to look around and find partners that have the know-how that they may lack; experience needed to go further together. It compels us to broaden our view, our scope of vision.

DRIVING CHANGE WITHIN THE CHAIN

Spontaneous initiatives from companies, universities and regions are often where alliance formation and Sharing Brainpower start. The European Commission has made this phenomenon the backbone of its industrial policy. It has set itself the goal of tackling the digital transition and the sustainability of society and economy in an integral way. By 2050, CO_2 emissions should be reduced to zero, with an intermediate goal of a 55% reduction by 2030.

Europe is unique in this approach, which is followed in the business world where intermediate goals are set. A growing group of companies is likewise striving to make their chains more sustainable. Suppliers of raw materials and packaging materials and the users of their products are involved in achieving the reduction of CO_2.

Two examples: the Board of PepsiCo has set itself the goal of emitting 40% less CO_2 by 2030. The management of the Dutch producer Van Lays, a subsidiary of PepsiCo, was stimulated by the objective and found a partner with which the production from gas to electricity can be realised. That partner is German startup Kraftblock, which has designed a battery that can store energy sustainably generated with sun and wind. By 2024, the conversion from natural gas to electricity should take place and CO_2 emissions should be reduced by 98%. The potato farmers are being consulted about structurally reducing the use of fertilisers and pesticides.

Heineken brews its beer in the Netherlands entirely with sustainable electricity. She does this in close consultation with her knowledge partner Eneco, which itself has wind farms in the North Sea. The main basic component is barley. Together with the farmers and the international food sector, work is being done to transparently make production more sustainable.

Two uniquely European 'building blocks of Sharing Brainpower' are very helpful in this process: first, the European Investment Bank, which can finance new initiatives and thus gives a positive signal to commercial financiers. And second, the national knowledge institutes of Applied Science, Fraunhofer, TNO, and others, which operate between universities and companies and have grown closer to the companies in recent years.

REGIONAL CONNECTIONS IN A TIME OF GLOBALISATION

Sharing Brainpower is often set up by companies and organisations that are already aware of each other by their proximity in a region. Initially, they may come up with initiatives that national policymakers have to find a way to fit into their policies. But now that Europe wants to combine the strengths of its member states and bring all the available know-how together for collective use, many regional bottom-up initiatives are getting a top-down boost.

Unlikely alliances

In The Netherlands, the Fieldlab *Campione* is researching 'Smart Maintenance.' Two companies were surprised to find each other there. But Tata Steel and Fuji Film appeared to have more in common than they had previously thought. They both work with conveyor belts to transport offset plates and steel. Since the rollers on these belts need to be periodically renewed but their moment of replacement is very unpredictable, Fuji approached Campione to find solutions. Campione was able to use existing data to build an algorithm for detecting the right time for replacement. This attracted the attention of Tata, for whom the same solution turned out to be available (World Class Maintenance, 2020).

CORONA, OUTSOURCING AND THE REGIONS

As we have seen from the case at Drachten, alliances can be a way to push back the trend of outsourcing activities. The Corona pandemic of 2020 made it clear to companies and politicians alike that outsourcing of production had led to complex international dependencies. Policy decisions, particularly by China, had major consequences for world trade. When the port of Shanghai was completely shut off, it resulted in long delays for container ships; the traffic of containers around the world was in complete disarray.

The lockdowns in Europe in 2020 resulted in a serious shrinking of economic activity. Forecasts were lowered and the ordering of parts, including chips from Asia, was dramatically reduced.

Modesty is required

A practical lesson from the Philips case in Drachten is that, as a prominent company (or multinational in a region), you cannot force your decisions on partners. Modesty and generosity are important. Siemens plays a vital role in all of the three EU transitions; but talks in Germany and the Netherlands have made it clear that SMEs do not want to find themselves in a position where they just have to go along with Siemens' decisions and goals. As the supplier of industrial IoT solution Mindsphere, the Siemens directorate took heed and is now working with smaller suppliers in the digital chain towards a well-functioning digital company network.

When the economy started to recover in late 2020, chip producers could not meet the sudden growth in demand. For the European Commission, this was a signal that the production of intelligent chips in Europe should now be speeded up. But setting up a new production capacity is expensive and complex.

The Corona pandemic exposed the vulnerability of the long supply lines which were partly a result of globalisation. Companies are now on the lookout for suppliers nearby. This change in direction also means that there are many new opportunities for Europeans regions to attract high-quality employment.

REFERENCE

World Class Maintenance (2020) Vijf jaar Fieldlab Campione brengt slim onderhoud binnen handbereik *(in Dutch)*. Available at https://www.worldclassmaintenance.com/vijf-jaar-fieldlab-campione-brengt-slim-onderhoudbinnen-handbereik/ (Accessed 5 September 2023).

CONCLUSIONS

EUROPE IS SLOWLY MATURING

In the Introduction, I mentioned a heated discussion between a director of the Bundesbank and a senior representative of the Franch Ministry of Economics and Finance. It was not the start of a diplomatic war, because the rules of the game were described within the EMS. In hindsight, I witnessed the birth of a new Europe: parties could disagree without starting a war. In the past 40 years this sense of a new Europe has grown more mature. The united support Ukraine received was a landmark: European sovereignty was no longer an abstract vision. The war Russia started was felt as a common threat; an aggression that had to be averted.

Before, Europe lived under the impression that its model of soft power, harmony and human rights would suffice for all its endeavours. But the cold reality is that the world around us is changing radically and that our way of working, too, must change. Covid and the war in Ukraine have taught policymakers that Europe is too dependent on Russian oil and gas and on cheap and smart manufacturing power in China. But we have also found out that our post-war ally America with its protectionist climate policy is blocking our goals.

Europe must become more assertive and follow its own course. This is a slow cultural and social process – but we are making

DOI: 10.4324/9781032703381-24

headway. Ultimately, we have to stand on our own two feet and for that, radical political choices have to be made.

The policies implemented by the European Commission are mainly technological in nature; the three transitions should lead to more sustainability, an end to the use to fossil fuels and an accelerated digitisation of society and economy. In the first phase in which the transitions are now, frictions become visible, because on top of old structures and dated legislation, new initiatives are perceived as limiting. Resistance and misunderstanding, on the one hand, and criticism that we are divesting of polluting products too slowly, on the other, are the logical consequences.

For the environmental movement, the end of our dependence on fossil fuels cannot come fast enough. But the economic reality is that more and more countries are striving for more prosperity, which means energy, which means (fossil) fuel. Europe must be able to respond to this ambiguity.

The European Commission has opted for Sharing Brainpower, rightly assuming that the pooling of knowledge will lead to strength and solidarity and to new sustainable technologies. But its own contribution, the granting of state aid, has so far been limited, so as not to disrupt the internal market. This choice is in stark contrast to the extensive state support given in China and the USA to create sustainable global players. The commission has rightly, if temporarily, provided more room for state aid to new digital initiatives and wind energy, under political pressure from Germany and France.

Europe operates globally from a position of disadvantage. EU innovation policy was first explicitly mentioned as recently as 2010, and thenceforth provided with a growing budget. What is still missing in Europe is a 'winning mentality' that recognises the disadvantage, but expresses the drive and self-belief to convert that disadvantage into a lead. In Denmark, Ørsted's management has shown that the state-owned energy company can make a double turn: from fossil to wind and from state to private company. In Sweden, ex-Tesla employee Peter Carlsson was able to quickly establish a battery factory with Northvolt. He wants to show

Europe that not only the Americans are capable of this. Sharing Brainpower is a unique tool that Europe has at its disposal; a tool that the Americans and Chinese look at with some jealousy.

TECH COMPANIES WANT RULES AND REGULATIONS

European government can be somewhat wavering. The technical know-how is there, but the opportunism and courage of the entrepreneur is missing at crucial moments. Their stance is like company management technically perfecting a new development, because in their view the customer is not ready for (or willing to accept) an imperfect product. This is reminiscent of the technical managers at Nokia and Ericsson, who were global leaders at the time but lost the market to 'quick and dirty' Asian innovation.

For a moment it seemed that with the recent AI innovations, Europe would again fall behind international competition. But in this field, too, knowledge in Europe is as much advanced as in the USA. It was OpenAI, with the support of Microsoft, that quickly released ChatGPT, a web app that independently produces texts in response to user questions. In a few months, hundreds of millions of people used the product. OpenAI CEO Sam Altman repeatedly stressed the immaturity of its product – but it was up and running anyway. In Europe, where technological innovations often come from scientific institutes, the emphasis is on perfecting the product before it enters the market.

But US tech companies that have developed without government intervention are now asking Washington for regulations to indicate the ethical limits that should apply to AI. In the USA, privacy legislation especially is increasingly seen as a special European strength. With its privacy legislation in 2018, Europe has already formulated rules on how companies handle the data they collect. Those who violate the rules can face a fine that can amount to tens of millions of euros.

Google CEO Sundar Pichai has advocated that Washington should follow Europe's lead, and lay down rules that designers can use as guides in the development of products such as ChatGPT.

Altman expressed a similar wish, to initiate a discussion about the limits of AI. Europe is indeed working on special legislation for AI, and the White House has made a first draft that the legislation should comply with.

In creating an industrial internet, Europe aims for a global standard, whereby the data remains the property of the companies that create it. Europe wants to give the same status to the data that must be stored in the European cloud. With calls from international tech companies themselves for clear regulations, the playing field changes dramatically. Cooperation with governments is suddenly deemed more necessary (and possible) than ever before; and Europe has the 'working model.'

CONDUCTOR OR MANAGING DIRECTOR?

In recent years, the European Commission has become the orchestra's conductor. Brussels can simplify and speed up the procedures of applying for aid. And the EC must quickly come up with an answer to the state support that the USA and China are giving to set up their own green industry. It does so by temporarily easing restrictions on state aid in order to preserve innovative companies in the wind energy and chip sectors.

But pressures remain between the European Commission and the European Council, in which heads of government of the member states take part. In the introduction, I described the three different ways in which technological-economic policy is shaped: the 'Nordic way,' the 'German Federative model' and the 'Paris Connection.' Though the actual routes taken may differ, what binds everyone in the European Council together is the conviction that the industrial policy of the 21st century must become more assertive, and that Sharing Brainpower must also be thought of in terms of power.

Europe has previously gained experience with this form of industrial policy; Airbus is a challenging example of this. After years of struggle and fragmentation that symbolised powerlessness, the knowledge that was scattered throughout Germany, France, England, the Netherlands, Italy and Spain was combined. French directive thinking, German Federative action and the Dutch/ Nordic drive to connect flowed together. It led to a world-class player in aviation.

EUROPEAN COMMISSION AS CONDUCTOR OF THE TRANSITIONS

If you look at how the world has changed over the last ten years and what still needs to change in the coming 20 years, the results can be overwhelming, to say the least. Plans and goals are so abstract that they are almost impossible to comprehend. It's impossible to divine a masterplan that can lay out the sequence of steps that have to be taken. With its Green Deal and the Corona Recovery Plan, the European Commission has taken impressive steps forward. But there are still many technological and scientific breakthroughs needed before we can definitively bid farewell to fossil fuels.

But gradually a new energy chain is being created. The success of offshore wind parks and sun-powered electricity has stimulated the local storage of excess electricity. A rapidly growing number of companies are active in this market segment. Tesla and Northvolt are active producers of home batteries. In 2019, Shell acquired the German startup Sonnen, which specialises in intelligent home batteries that are automatically connected with each other. In this way, a virtual power plant is constructed.

In 2017, the European Commission introduced its alliance strategy to address the shortage of much needed car batteries. They have become the conductor that has made alliance politics the core of its policy. Universities, institutions of applied science, local governments, companies, start-ups and technicians are pushed towards Sharing Brainpower. Together, in different and changing alliances, they can work on the scientific breakthroughs and technologies needed to make agriculture and industry sustainable in the coming decades.

In this way, Brussels is cleverly bringing the potential strengths of Europe together. The fragmentation that characterised the European project for so long is being turned into a strength. The network of Digital Innovation Hubs has started a process of connecting strengths in cities and in the regions. In countries which have not built up a tradition of applied science institutes, universities can take on this role. The dynamic from the supply side of the economy is consciously stimulated, not left to markets alone.

CONDITIONS FOR SOUND DIRECTORSHIP

With its industry policy, Europe has made its first steps towards greater international autonomy. But Brussels has to lead the transitions towards further digitalisation, sustainability and innovation with firm and clear steps. That requires a number of conditions. I will sum up the most important here.

1 – Intermediate steps for energy transition recommended

The long-term path to energy transition has been set out with the Green Deal and the plans for the construction of a European battery chain. With these initiatives, Brussels has sketched the contours of future markets on which entrepreneurs and scientists can focus. But there is a lot of work needed by the European Commission. Investors, entrepreneurs, politicians and scientists are still waiting for clarity on how 'green' electricity must be.

But 'long-term' is the key word here. The question is, How long can natural gas and nuclear energy be used and under which conditions? When it comes to nuclear energy, it's not a matter of the energy itself being green or not – because it is not. The question must be whether nuclear waste is or can be made green.

For the short term, a growing group of countries see nuclear energy as a way to achieve a reduction in CO_2 emissions. In France, nuclear power plants are still responsible for 70% of electricity generation. Zero CO_2 emissions, but long-lasting nuclear waste. In many other countries, particularly in central Europe – Poland, the Czech Republic, Slovakia, Hungary, Romania and Slovenia – there are plans to build new nuclear plants. They, too, will lead to a reduction in CO_2 emissions – but nuclear waste will become a growing problem.

A solution for nuclear waste?

How can the problem of nuclear waste be tackled? In the municipality of Mol in Belgium, the nuclear study centre Studiecentrum Kernenergie (SCK) is working on a new nuclear reactor which uses existing nuclear waste as its fuel.

Professor Hamid Ait Abderrahim, who leads the Centre, is convinced that the problem of nuclear waste can be solved. The reactor is powered by a particle accelerator. At present building costs amount to 1.6 billion euros. The federal Belgian government has invested 558 million euros into the project, which is expected to be ready in 2026 (Abderrahim, 2022).

To develop the plant to an industrial level will require further billions. Belgium is looking for financial and technical research partners to work on the project (which can also be adapted for cancer treatment). It is a challenge for Brussels to get this Sharing Brainpower-project off the ground financially, to bring the sustainability of nuclear energy one step closer.

Natural gas as a transitional fuel has many advantages but Brussels should be more precise in its requirements. There should be a timeline for making CO_2 capture compulsory. At the same time, the re-use of CO_2 must be stimulated. With its measures for the re-use of nuclear waste and CO_2, the EU can lead science and companies to new markets.

2 – Government data as key to digital transition

The main reason for building the International Data Space (IDS) and the European cloud Gaia-X is to win back data sovereignty. Politicians have rightly expressed their concern over the fact that the storage of data by (mainly) American data companies means too much (commercial) power is given away. The growing digitalisation of government, companies and organisations gives these data storage companies considerable potential power. There is a role here for Brussels when it comes to the further development and exploitation of IDS and Gaia-X, and in the negotiations with non-European data companies. It can use the fact that governments are the leading clients for these services as a trump card.

3 – Government's buying power to stimulate innovation

Governments are increasingly more active in financially supporting research that leads to new products. But another way to further innovation is not used enough by the government: it can stimulate research by proposing use cases, or stimulate business by ordering and buying new products. Daan Kersten, CEO of PhotonFirst, which integrates photonic chips in tension and temperature measuring systems, says it would be a big help if the government bought the measuring systems as a 'launching customer.' The government would receive a new tool to, say, make the maintenance of infrastructure more predictable; the young company can balance its research and business sides, and lower their entrance barrier to new customers.

Of course, there is the risk that the government's purchase could create unfair competition on the market. It is up to Brussels to set the limits.

4 – Clear and practical guidelines

Europe's ambition is for its industry and agriculture to be circular in 2050. The long road to achieve this needs markers along the way, similar to the clear rules laid down in the Paris Accord. These state, for example, the guidelines which project developers and architects work to; how much CO_2 emissions per square metre is permitted. There are also agreements that this limit will gradually be reduced over time (see, for instance, Lynch, 2021).

It is Brussels' turn to present clear rules and reward farmers and industrial companies who are prepared to work in a circular, and therefore more sustainable, way. Those not adhering to the rules or working against them should be penalised.

5 – Protecting industry from a too-speedy transition

The creation of a level playing field in the EU took a hit in 2021, during the Climate summit in Glasgow. A proposal from England, the USA, Canada and Denmark wanted to ban government subsidies for fossil fuels. The rest of the participating countries agreed to this for coal mining. A smaller group – 26 countries including the Netherlands – were also in favour of scrapping the subsidy for gas and oil production. China, South Korea and Japan did not sign, and neither did Germany, France, Italy and Belgium.

The consequence of this scraping subsidy is that, for instance, dredging companies such as Dutch Boskalis are unable to insure their activities. Export credit insurance for major dredging projects, especially in the framework of gas and oil production, is crucial. The level playing field within Europe – between the Netherlands and Belgium – and with Asian parties, is now disrupted.

Brussels, which was a prominent participant in Glasgow, could not prevent this unequal growth. There is now a hot dossier on the cards for the commission to iron out this uneven situation before 2023 – the date on which the regulation comes into force.

UNEASY RELATIONSHIP BETWEEN BRUSSELS AND MEMBER STATES

The new role of the European Commission must not be confused with the return of the strong state, much as it may be the vision of France, in particular. The role of the European Commission as I see it, is that of initiator, director and controller of transition policy. The EC asks member states to formulate policy that leads to sustainability, digitalisation and innovation. The EC does not impose this policy but is nevertheless often seen as 'the civil servants in Brussels laying down a dictate.'

Where this discussion does in fact apply, is in another role that the European Council has moved from the government leaders to the commission: that of the enforcer of democratic values such as freedom of expression and the independence of the courts. Since 2013, Hungary has introduced legislation that severely limits both these values. Since 2017, the Polish government has followed the same policy of limiting these values.

Hungary and Poland express their opposition to Brussels both verbally and in terms of policy. They accuse politicians from other countries of wanting to create a federal Europe with their megalomanic plans. For them looms a picture of sombre times from the Soviet era or, even worse, they accuse the Germans of still wanting to build a Third Reich.

As part of the conditions which member states must meet in order to qualify for money from the emergency fund, the member states have demanded that the European Commission look at whether countries comply with rules on press freedom and an independent judiciary. The European Court has been asked whether the commission can use this instrument, and they decided that this is possible.

In a presentation for the European Parliament, the Polish Prime Minister Matheusz Marowiecki stated that his government sees Europe as a union of sovereign states and that the European Court cannot put itself above Polish legislation. An interesting statement because by doing so, the prime minister is introducing a bipolar situation. He sees the EU as an alliance of states and as such puts himself at odds with the wishes of 'the others' who want to grow towards a federation. But the fact is that Poland has voted for the primacy of the European Court but does not want to accept it.

The discussion on further integration must take place in an open way, without the preconceived goal of a federation. That is not in keeping with the character of the European cooperation. By joining the EU, every country by definition surrenders sovereignty.

For decades the EU has tried to ensure that the institutional adjustments that are needed for further integration are done in a democratic way. For example, after the major expansion of the EU at the beginning of this century, it was decided in Lisbon that a large number of topics in the European Council no longer required unanimous agreement but that weighted majority was sufficient.

An ultimate goal in this process was never defined. The direction of the integration will be determined by what circumstances demand.

PERSONAL APPROACH

The strong growth of the European Union in the first decade of this century has resulted in 27 member states. A number of candidates in the Balkans are warming up for imminent membership. Serbia, Bosnia-Herzegovina, North Macedonia, Kosovo and Albania have expressed their desire to join the European Union. The war that raged in former Yugoslavia during the 1990s had left deep scars. In the end, Europe needed the diplomatic and military powers of the USA to establish peace.

The ethnic and religious diversity of the Balkans calls for intelligent soft power to prevent a new war. The candidate countries want to be heard; China and Russia are playing on this desire. If it is paid to do so, Beijing is offering to improve infrastructure or revive old industries in, for example, Serbia. In Montenegro, China is building a motorway. Russia, however, is spreading division by disinformation.

Next to the traditional civil service and political procedures for moving closer, a personal approach is needed. Someone is needed to guide the membership of these West Balkan countries, not as separate parties but as one entity. These countries should not have the feeling that they are being kept on a leash, or that their membership is a back-up plan. Respect and discipline are needed. And we must work towards a deadline for their membership.

Brexit gave the European Commission experience with a negotiator who guided the process. From 2016 to 2021, Michel Barnier was the listening ear in the capitals of all the member states and he learnt how to deal with the constantly changing political tensions in London. When an agreement was reached and he presented it in the European Parliament, there was a round of applause for Barnier after the debate. It is high time that the European Commission sets up a 'reverse Brexit strategy' for the West Balkans and appoints an appropriate envoy to manage the task.

A MORE DECISIVE FOREIGN POLICY

Current European political issues weigh heavy on the success of the three transitions that run through this book. The war in Ukraine, in particular, teaches Europe that it must be able to make a fist. The question is whether Europe will do this on its own or as an autonomous unit within NATO? The former Soviet states have the greatest confidence in the effectiveness of the USA and opt for a strong autonomous position within NATO. France, traditionally, does not want to be on the leash of the USA and wants the EU to opt for its own sovereignty and therefore for its own army. Another question on the Brussels agenda is how Europe sees its future relationship with Russia.

Europe is being bombarded with disinformation and computer hacks from Russia. There are attempts to break into the computer systems of institutions, companies and governments. At the same time, Russia claims that its neighbour Ukraine has no rights as an independent state because its land was originally Russian. Putin ultimately wants to reestablish the Soviet Union.

The geopolitical issues sketched above are a big influence on each of the three transitions, digital, energy and CO_2, and on the speed and direction of Europe's innovative powers. The decisiveness of the EU's transition policy is also (partly) dependent on a decisive foreign policy and a tough stance when it comes to the political situation in the Balkans. Some suggestions:

1 – European defence must get an extra financial impulse

Europe has been dependent on NATO for its security for a long time. Now that the USA is turning its focus of attention on Asia, the EU is becoming aware that a sound, shared security policy has become its own responsibility.

European government leaders are still averse to talking about setting up a European army, even though Angela Merkel already has raised the issue during her tenure as German head of state. After Russia attacked Ukraine, Macron's old plan for setting up a raid intervention force was put into practice. The question is how the coordination of this force will be directed. Germany has established a Darpa-type institute that is dedicated to new digital instruments and software. The aim is to reduce the dependence on non-European software and hardware suppliers.

Europe must work on developing its own ears and eyes on the ground and in the air. To do this, we must set up our own network of satellites and drones. This will be a long-running, expensive project; the equipment must be made in Europe. A considerable financial effort is required to support such a defence policy.

2 – Setting up a European Security Council

Like Russia, China is also carrying out a disinformation campaign against Europe. Also, China's investments in Europe, such as the takeover of a part of the port of Piraeus in Greece, lead to new dependencies, making Europe's international sanctions policy toothless. An attempt to respond to China's human rights violations in the Muslim province of Xinjiang with sanctions has already been blocked by a Greek veto.

Europe needs a system change that will make its foreign policy more decisive. This is all the more necessary if the European Union becomes larger with the admission of the six West Balkan countries. This means that current member states must give up some of their sovereignty. In an interview with *Frankfurter Allgemeine Zeitung*, former German chancellor Merkel floated the idea that Europe could set up a Security Council with a few permanent members and rotating membership for the other member states. This seems like a smart idea.

3 – The EU should not become a fort

Corona considerably restricted the free movement of people. With its zero-tolerance policy, the Factory of the World closed its gates. Politicians and businesses in the USA and Europe realised that outsourcing sometimes went too far when the simplest of resources, such as face masks, were only made in China.

Producing products locally, in close proximity to consumers, is rediscovered. This makes sense not just economically; robotisation and 3D-printing also make global trade less of an automatic solution. This development calls for a mindset that is in line with the industry policy that the commission has in mind: Sharing Brainpower in 'forgotten' regions is preferable to outsourcing work to cheap labour countries.

In the last few years, Europe has taken measures to limit the sale of strategically important companies to non-European owners. For an economic bloc that has always profited from open borders and multilateral treaties to regulate the movement of trade and capital, the unilateral imposition of these measures is a break with the past.

The idea is not to build a Fort Europe. But to do business here, outsiders must comply with the conditions which apply in the biggest and wealthiest consumer market in the world. Europe itself has to get used to the new situation in which negotiations are carried out on the basis of the standards we use.

THE EU CAN BECOME A FOUNTAIN OF KNOWLEDGE

Early in this century, government leaders decided policy in the coming decade should stimulate a 'knowledge economy.' This was in the era that entrepreneurs, politicians and researchers were rushing off to Silicon Valley to experience for themselves the energy that was taking over that part of the world. How new firms were moving forward, how financiers were talking about their investment plans in roadside cafes, how researchers were hatching their start-up plans at Stanford University. We Europeans could not believe our eyes.

The bureaucratic text of the European leaders' Lisbon Treaty was in sharp contrast to the reality in California. But much has changed for the better in Europe over the last 20 years. When I began research for my previous book in 2012, universities were reluctantly beginning to set up departments to help students start their own business. Financiers kept their distance from these sorts of initiatives and national governments only reluctantly expanded the funds that financed these innovations.

But developments have accelerated in the last five years. Paris, Berlin, Stockholm, London and Amsterdam have been discovered by venture capitalists. Every university has its own incubator where young entrepreneurs are guided. A growing number of graduates want to work at a start-up rather than at the traditional major corporation.

Europe sees universities as an important source for the commercialisation of knowledge. That is understandable and useful. But there is also risk involved in this development: a source can become exhausted if it cannot replenish itself. Fundamental scientific research is vital. For this, enough resources must be made available, for a long time. In this way, researchers do not have to be experts in getting subsidies or leave to go somewhere where money is plentiful.

Universities then can become magnets that will attract and keep talented minds. This is a necessary condition for Europe to become a fountain of knowledge.

REFERENCES

Abderrahim, H.A. (2022) MYRRHA: An accelerator driven system to manage radioactive waste. Available at https://www.iaea.org/bulletin/myrrha-an-accelerator-driven-system-to-manage-radioactive-waste (Accessed 5 September 2023).

Lynch, C. (2021) The Construction Industry Is Getting Greener: Why, How, And What's Changing? Available at https://www.forbes.com/sites/sap/2021/08/25/the-construction-industry-is-getting-greener-why-how-and-whats-changing/ (Accessed 5 September 2023).

BIBLIOGRAPHY OF WORKS USED

BOOKS

Blom, P. (2018) *Wat op het spel staat.* Amsterdam, De Bezige Bij.

Blom, P. (2019) *De duizelingwekkende jaren. Europa 1900–1914.* Amsterdam, De Bezige Bij.

Bollmann, R. (2021) *Angela Merkel: De kanselier en haar tijd.* Amsterdam, De Arbeiderspers. Dutch translation of Angela Merkel: Die Kanzlerin und Ihre Zeit. München, C.H. Beck.

Christensen, C.M. (1997) *The Innovator's Dilemma: When new technologies cause great firms to fail.* Boston, MA, Harvard Business Review Press.

Clark, C. (2015) *Slaapwandelaars: Hoe Europa in 1914 ten oorlog trok.* Amsterdam, De Bezige Bij.

Clissold, T. (2005) *Mr. China: A memoir.* New York, Harper Business.

Domingos, P. (2018) *The master algorithm.* New York, Basic Books.

Frankopan, P. (2016) *De Zijderoutes.* Houten, Spectrum.

Garton Ash, T. (2023) *Homelands: A personal history of Europe.* London, The Bodley Head.

Greeven, M.J., Wei, W. (2017) *Business ecosystems in China.* New York, Routledge.

Greeven, M.J., Yip, G.S., Wei Wei (2019) *Pioneers, hidden champions, changemakers, and underdogs.* Cambridge, MA, The MIT Press.

Harari, Y.N. (2011) *Sapiens: A brief history of humankind.* London, Vintage Books.

Harari, Y.N. (2018) *21 lessons for the 21st century.* London, Spiegel & Grau.

Katz, B., Nowak, J. (2018) *The new localism: How cities can thrive in the age of populism.* Washington, DC, Brookings Institution Press.

Kay-Fu, L. (2018) *AI Superpowers: China, Silicon Valley and the new world order.* New York, Houghton Mifflin Harcourt.

Mulgan, G. (2018) *Big Mind: How collective intelligence can change our world.* Princeton, NJ, Princeton University Press.

Ries, E. (2011) *The Lean Startup: How today's entrepreneurs use continuous innovation to create radically successful businesses.* New York, Crown Business.

Roelens, G. (2013) *How successful can you be in China? A recipe for success.* Tielt, Lannoo.

Schulte Nordholt, H. (2016) *China en de Barbaren: Het verzet tegen de westerse wereldorde.* Amsterdam, Querido.

Schulte Nordholt, H. (2021) *Is China nog te stoppen? Hoe een virus de wereldorde verandert.* Amsterdam, Querido.

Smit, J. (2019) *Het Grote Gevecht & Het eenzame gelijk van Paul Polman.* Amsterdam, Prometheus.

Uittenbogaard, P. (2018) *Detroit: Ontwaken uit de Amerikaanse nachtmerrie.* Den Haag, Vitabrevis.

Walt, S.M. (2018) *The Hell of Good Intentions: America's foreign policy elite and the decline of US primacy.* New York, Farrar, Straus, and Giroux.

Wijk, R. de (2019) *De Nieuwe Wereldorde: Hoe China sluipenderwijs de macht overneemt.* Amsterdam, Balans.

ARTICLES

Bakker, F. (2016) Buren en vrienden houden Europa spiegel voor. *Het Financieele Dagblad*, August 17, 2016.

Bakker, F. (2016) De 3D-musketiers. *Het Financieele Dagblad*, February 2, 2016.

Bakker, F. (2018) De herwaardering van het ambacht. *Het Financieele Dagblad*, June 15, 2018.

Bakker, F. (2018) Overal wordt gebouwd aan allianties. *Het Financieele Dagblad*, July 14, 2018.

Bakker, F. (2018) The EU can win the war on technology. Euractiv.com, October 5, 2018.

Blumenthal, D., Chopra, A. (2018) Apple's pact with 13 health care systems might actually disrupt the industry. *Harvard Business Review*, March 23, 2018.

Brynjolfsson, E. (2022) The Turing Trap. Stanford University, Digital Economy Lab.

Damm, D. (2017) As machines take jobs, companies need to get creative about making new ones. *Harvard Business Review*, May 22, 2017.

Deichmann, D., Rozentaler, I., Barnhoorn, R. (2017) Open innovation generates great ideas, so why aren't companies adopting them? *Harvard Business Review*, December 20, 2017.

Finn, E. (2018) A smarter way to think about intelligent machines. *The New York Times*, November 5, 2018.

Goby, N., Brandt, T., Neumann, D. (2018) How a German manufacturing company set up its analytics lab. *Harvard Business Review*, November 2, 2018.

Higgins, A. (2017) Russia wants innovation, but it's arresting its innovators. *The New York Times*, August 9, 2017.

Lohr, S. (2018) China extends lead as the most prolific supercomputer maker. *The New York Times*, June 25, 2018.

Lutchen, K.R. (2018) Why companies and universities should forge long-term collaborations. *Harvard Business Review*, January 24, 2018.

Lyles, W., Berke, P., Heiman-Overstreet, K. (2017) Cities should start small when adapting to climate change. *Harvard Business Review*, November 2017.

McKinsey Global Institute (2016) The age of analytics: Competing in a data-driven world. McKinsey, December 2016.

Metz, C. (2018) Mark Zuckerberg, Elon Musk and the feud over killer robots. *The New York Times*, June 9, 2018.

Metz, C. (2018) The next tech talent shortage: Quantum computing researchers. *The New York Times*, October 21, 2018.

Metz, C., Zhong, R. (2018) The race is on to protect data from the next leap in computers. And China has the lead. *The New York Times*, December 3, 2018.

Mitchell, M. (2018) Artificial Intelligence hits the barrier of meaning. *The New York Times*, November 5, 2018.

Posen, B.R. (2019) Trump aside, can US still fit in NATO? *The New York Times*, March 12, 2019.

Wilson, J.H., Daugherty, P.R., Davenport, C. (2019) The future of AI will be about less data, not more. *Harvard Business Review*, January 14, 2019.

Yi-Zheng, L. (2019) Where spying is the law. *The New York Times*, March 13, 2019.

Yuan, L. (2018) China's tech industry from a Silicon Valley perspective. *The New York Times*, November 5, 2018.

Yuan, L. (2018) Why Made in China 2025 will succeed, despite Trump. *The New York Times*, July 4, 2018.

Yuan, L. (2018) ZTE's near-collapse may be China's sputnik moment. *The New York Times*, June 10, 2018.

ACKNOWLEDGEMENTS

While writing this book, I was regularly asked if I was working with Antoine van Agtmael again. I explained why this was not the case: After our first book, Antoine had promised his wife *The Smartest Places on Earth* would be his last one. They happily spent their time together, visiting good friends in Japan and India, among other places.

He did provide this book with a Foreword, in which he kindly calls my work a 'call for action' to entrepreneurs, scientists and policy makers; a call to maximize the European innovative powers.

In this book, I dive deeper into the concept of 'Sharing Brainpower', the concept we coined in our first book together. But I soon found out that I missed Antoine's quick and focused thinking. In Pim van Tol, the editor of the Dutch version of our first book, I found the sparring partner I needed. In his home town of Rotterdam we regularly met, rather fittingly, at the Hotel New York, a historic connection point between Europe and America. I was able to express my thoughts on how I would or would not want to proceed, thereby conjuring up the necessary inspiration and drive. He listened and asked questions. Pim's experience in international publishing eventually led to a deal with Routledge.

From the beginning, I was convinced that the book should be published in English. Mark Fuller and Abi Daruvalla, friends and former colleagues, took on the task of translating an earlier version of this manuscript, for which I am greatly indebted.

With the expert help of Niels Hartog, I have set up an accompanying website, sharingbrainpower.eu. Here, the theme of Sharing Brainpower is further established, with many working cases, the latest facts and figures and some additional insights. I hope this will be a continuing work in progress.

An earlier version of the manuscript was also presented to Ed Groot and Rien Van Lent, who provided valuable criticism that allowed me to state many points much clearer. Principally, they convinced me to steer the book away from the global War for Technology, towards a specifically European approach: How does it work, and what is so special about it?

In my many years as a journalist at *Het Financieele Dagblad* in Amsterdam, I was very happy with the opportunity to speak to prominent entrepreneurs, scientists, bankers and politicians. Over the years, I gradually saw their attitude change. Their initial skepticism and cynicism about climate change and sustainability gave way to sincere worries and a sense of reality.

I thank the European Commission for showing the courage to stop the depletion of the Earth. In this book, I describe what profound scientific and social adjustments are necessary to ensure we all can live in continued comfort with sustainable products.

I also want to thank all the people I have spoken to in the Eindhoven region, who have increased my understanding of Sharing Brainpower. Egbert-Jan Sol opened the door to his colleagues at TNO; John Blankendaal showed me how an industrial campus should work, Daan Kersten did not tire of thinking about successful alliances and Arnold Stokking showed me how chemistry and agriculture can become sustainable.

Finally, I dedicate this book to Frances, my wife, who sometimes grew tired of hearing all the storylines that came to mind. And to Jake and Duco, my two grandsons born in London, who will help shape the future I describe.

INDEX

For Product Safety Concerns and Information please contact our EU representative GPSR@taylorandfrancis.com
Taylor & Francis Verlag GmbH, Kaufingerstraße 24, 80331 München, Germany

www.ingramcontent.com/pod-product-compliance
Lightning Source LLC
LaVergne TN
LVHW021128300926
849160LV00010B/921
9781032703374